tchwork

WITHDRAWN
University Libraries
University of Memphis

[Robertson, Katherine (Copeland)]

To Richmond

Violet Bank

Bridge

Harbor

The Market

Court House

To City Point

Centre Hill Mansion

Blandford Church

Confederate Memorial

ater Road

The Crater

Ginna Sarman

BRAVEST SURRENDER

A Petersburg Patchwork

PETERSBURG TODAY — *The city shows few scars of the battles which have raged in and around it since Fort Henry was erected in 1645 following an Indian massacre. From this point, on May 10, 1781, Lafayette shelled Petersburg which was then occupied by the British.*

BRAVEST SURRENDER

A Petersburg Patchwork

❀

by

CATHERINE COPELAND

Illustrated with Photographs by

P. HAIRSTON SEAWELL

❀

1961

THE PRESS OF WHITTET & SHEPPERSON

RICHMOND, VIRGINIA

THIS BOOK IS DEDICATED
WITH ADMIRATION AND DEVOTION
TO
CALVIN BRAGG VALENTINE
HONORARY PRESIDENT
THE COLONIAL DAMES OF AMERICA
IN THE STATE OF VIRGINIA

❁

FOREWORD

PETERSBURG, a dowager among cities, has many charms. Founded over 300 years ago, the city has attracted innumerable friends and too many foes. Invaded and captured, defended and surrendered, Petersburg conceals her scars gracefully. As with good wine, Petersburg has a bouquet. All-pervading is the richness of the tobacco warehouses — a reminder of past wealth. But the true bouquet is the lemony fragrance of magnolias. This flower of Southern Belles is particularly the favored blossom of Petersburg, where its trees attain noteworthy size.

Petersburg has taste. The ancestral mahogany dining board woos the appetite of any guest with Virginia dishes, gracefully served after generations of testing.

Petersburg has style. Aged brick, columned houses, iron fences, boxwood walks — compose a pleasant, if haphazard, picture. The pattern, architecturally, ranges from stone of the early settlers to brick of the Colonial, assorted columns of Classic Revival, stucco and gingerbread of the Victorian. These mixed styles sit serenely side by side in neighborly fashion.

Petersburg has people. And what a population! Pocahontas knew it as home. George Washington and Lafayette were favored guests. Its Revolutionary sons fought for it. Its children and old men went forth together in Petersburg's most heroic hour to hold off its enemy. General Lee fought in it. Here he became Commander-in-chief of the Confederate forces, and surrendered the city at the last. General Grant fought for it, taking it at last. Here Carrie Nation was rejected and William Makepeace Thackeray was ignored.

The years unfold. The paths of Fate cross and recross. The manners of the forest give way to creeping civilization. Gentility and culture join hands at this crossroads of American history. A way of life is born — suffers, fades, and nearly expires. Now it breathes more slowly, but no less gracefully. Petersburg carries on.

Some years ago historical interest carried me to Petersburg. Its charm captured me and I indulged an avocation for photography. Only a few years before, the path of a native of Petersburg had circled back. After years spent elsewhere — many devoted to writing — the author of this book came home. With devotion, Catherine Copeland began the story she knew so well.

The character of a place — as of a person — is often revealed in many small incidents. This is particularly true of Petersburg, whose noble place in history is well known and frequently recounted. Miss Kate set about the portrayal of the subtle and lesser known side of this lady of cities.

These stories are, with some small exception, not of Catherine Copeland, but those of Petersburg. They are, however, the author's stories — whether of earlier eras or of her early days. These are stories of happiness and sorrow — of excitement and glory. They are history.

Having mutual friends, Miss Kate and I met. With the same interest drawing us to Petersburg our separate ventures became a collaboration. We made notes using a fence rail as a desk. We shared ideas over delectable batterbread. We toasted the future, and drank of the past. Together we explored this legendary city. But our adventures during this time are stories for a future day. We must look back for the day of Petersburg's greatest glory. Then a manner of living was disrupted. It was then that Destiny decreed that bravest surrender.

P. Hairston Seawell

Petersburg,
7 May 1961

IN APPRECIATION

MY THANKS to my collaborator, P. Hairston Seawell, who brought this book into focus; to Edward A. Wyatt, IV, for reading the manuscript, and for his invaluable criticism; to Theresa D. Hodges, former Librarian of the Petersburg Public Library, and members of the Staff for their constant assistance.

My gratitude for comment and contribution to James H. Clark, Jr., Benjamin Mason Hill, Jr., Walter T. McCandlish, Clary S. Mullen, James Mullen, Miss Isabel L. Walker; and to the *Richmond Times-Dispatch* for permission to reprint "Christmas."

And thanks, most of all, to the dear old city herself. Petersburg supplied the patches — I only did the feather-stitching.

CATHERINE COPELAND

Petersburg, 1960

CONTENTS

❀

COVER DESIGN: *From a patchwork quilt made in Petersburg by ancestress of the author.*

END PAPERS: *A patchwork map of Petersburg by Ginna Jarman.*

LIST OF ILLUSTRATIONS

✿

A people is, in the last analysis,
        a repertory of customs.   JOSE ORTEGA Y GASSET

FOLLY CASTLE — Peter Jones, descendant of the Peter Jones for whom Petersburg is named, was a bachelor when he built this handsome Georgian town house in 1763. Because of its size the house was considered a "folly."

PETERSBURG: *A Profile*

❀

"AST IS PROLOGUE"
These words written on the National Archives Building, in Washington, were read aloud slowly, and with an interrogation at the end, by two tourists. The cab driver, hastening to dispel the mist, said: "Mister, that's Government talk for you ain't seen nothing yet!"

Perhaps nowhere in our country is the past more present than in Petersburg. It has been said that there is more history to the square foot than in any other city in the United States.

It is history televised, and in color.

It is red men slipping through the tall pines in the early days of the colonists; it is red coats swarming through the streets in the Revolution; it is gray coats in 1861; blue coats in '65; khaki clad lads at Camp Lee in the First World War; the same soldiers with different faces at Fort Lee today.

It is miles of battlefields, poignant, eloquent; breastworks shadowed now by giant pines where the blue and the gray sweated it out for nine long months; the "Crater" with its "dark and bloody ground." Petersburg not only has a Battlefield Park — it *is* a battlefield. It has been marched over, fought over, cried over, died over, for three hundred years.

Petersburg is not only a place — it is a personality.

It is comfortable old houses flanked by tall magnolias — exclamation points to dramatize the white clapboards and warm red brick.

It is iron fences with crape myrtle waving pink plumes of welcome; it is wistaria flung up in trees, spilling down in a purple fountain.

It is delicate iron work crocheted around porches and windows; wide stone steps leading up to old doorways with ruby and sapphire glass running around them like red and blue ribbons. It is the train who-who-ooo-oo-ing in the night; it is the warm smell of tobacco and molasses, a sweet rhapsody in brown.

It is old Blandford Church; it is going out on the 9th of June to decorate the graves of Confederate soldiers with the Stars and Bars.

It is rambling streets — one rambles longer than any in this country they say — Halifax Street rambles plumb down to Louisiana! New Orleans, anyone?

It is Christmas behind holly-wreathed doors with eggnog and beaten biscuits and ham and fruit cake, made by a recipe that has been handed down with as much reverence as the portrait of the lady who first made it.

It is box-bordered "gyardens" with the Harrison roses, and larkspur and wallflower, with hollyhock ladies peeping over the fence. And magnolias, always magnolias, satin in the sun, velvet in the moonlight.

We are told that it takes three generations to make a gentleman. But it takes three centuries to make a lady — a great lady like Petersburg.

She was just a little thing in 1645. But she grew fast, and soon (with Indians slipping in and out of the stockade for an extra thrill) she began flirting with Peter Jones. A frisky, young piece she was, but in 1733 Peter gave her his name, she settled down to home-making, and that's what she's been doing for two hundred years.

Yes, Petersburg is an old lady. Not one of those frizzy old ladies with her face lifted. No, indeed. She wears her lines and furrows with pride. And don't be fooled by the traffic and trucks and television. That is just the new look — neon lights making a jewelled necklace for her ample bosom. Underneath there beats the same old warm, sturdy heart.

For Petersburg is first of all a lady with a heart. Down in the mountains of North Carolina, where the first settlers in Petersburg established trade routes with the Cherokees, they have a word for a gracious hostess. They say: "Your house sits mighty easy. You won't never meet a stranger."

Petersburg is like that.

"You will never meet a stranger."

APPOMATTOX TO APPOMATTOX

❁

T WAS JUNE in Petersburg, 1864.

The quiet, dignified old houses brooded behind their iron fences; the air was sweet with magnolias. Then the storm burst. Suddenly the air was filled with shrieking shells. First, the Old Market was hit, then Bollingbrook Street, and Sycamore as far as Washington, was ablaze.

The Siege of Petersburg, "unparalleled in this or any other war," had begun. It was to continue for three hundred dreadful days.

The strategy of the war converged on Petersburg. General Grant was moving against Richmond; General Lee was protecting Richmond, Petersburg was in between. It was the back door to the Confederacy's capital.

General Grant, after he failed to take the city by assault (and historians still wonder why) settled down to his "grindstone policy." He made his headquarters at Appomattox Manor, at City Point.

This action, called by Dr. Arthur Kyle Davis — "The greatest hammer and rapier duel in history — Grant's sledge hammer blows dented, but did not crush the defense, and Lee's rapier thrusts could reach no vital part of the opponent's line. Grant had to 'move back by the left,' and Lee's line stretched so long as to break."

Dr. Davis adds, "Not Waterloo, nor Gettysburg is more sacred ground."

On the 18th of June, Petersburg had the Army of the Potomac staring it in the face. General Grant's magnificent army was one hundred thousand strong, "with all the world to recruit from."

By the 19th of June the Siege had begun. The Confederates dug in, "they exchanged the musket for the spade" — and axes and bayonets, knives, every utensil they could find — to dig the twenty-three miles of trenches that encircled the city.

Thirteen pitched battles were fought in and around these trenches, besides innumerable skirmishes and minor engagements.

The most spectacular, of course, was the Battle of the Crater, fought on the 30th of July, 1864. The great mine which exploded under the Confederates' works was supposed to end the Confederacy. Instead "this fiasco of the War," as it has been called, filled the city with casualties.

Hospitals were everywhere. Warehouses, public houses, private homes — what *wasn't* a hospital? The parks ran up the yellow flag, and the dead and the dying covered the grass.

When General Grant moved up, citizens of Petersburg moved out; some refugeed as far away as Lunenburg County.

As the months dragged on, however, many returned to ride out the storm. They built bomb-shelters in their yards and gardens, five or six feet deep, covered with heavy timbers and earth. Here the householder repaired until the heavy shelling, which generally lasted two or three hours, was over. Many of the old houses still show the bites taken by the hungry Union guns.

The Civil War, which we call the War Between the States, was called by Sir Winston Churchill "a war between gentlemen."

During the Siege, in the Crater area, between the trenches there was a large tree which seriously interfered with the field of fire of a Confederate gun. The Captain of the Battery asked for volunteers to go out and cut it down, even though it appeared that to do this was certain death.

A Petersburg boy, Sergeant Wesley Peyton Grigg, said he would obey orders to perform the mission, but could not volunteer as he did not think a Christian should deliberately commit suicide.

He was ordered to go. He went. And not a gun was fired from the Union lines until the tree fell! "A war between gentlemen."

But the ladies were in it too. During the Siege they nursed the sick, divided their scanty supplies of food and wine with the invalids, "irrespective of the color of the jacket."

Captain Gordon McCabe speaks of their "patient and calm endurance during the Siege" of Petersburg. He says: "Her men fitted to bear arms were yonder with Lee's veterans, and now her women suddenly environed by all the dread realities of war discovered a constancy and heroism befitting the wives and mothers of such valiant soldiers. They watched in hospitals, cheered on the convalescents, who when the sounds of battle grew nearer, rose like faithful soldiers to join their comrades, and others hurrying along

VIOLET BANK — In this house, now a part of Colonial Heights, General Lee, on July 18, 1864, established his headquarters. The ominous roar of the Crater explosion on July 30 must have rolled across the city to Violet Bank where the General occupied a tent on the lawn.

the deserted streets, the silence of which was ever and anon broken by a screaming shell, streamed out on the highways to meet the wounded and bear them to patriotic homes."

The city "girdled with fire and steel" struggled on through the weary weeks that ran into months. Then a "sense of casual peace" came into being. Adaptability, that protective coloring of the human spirit, took over. A business-as-usual policy was inaugurated. True, there wasn't much business; they said they went out with a basket full of money and brought back their purchases in their hands!

But trading went on. And in war, as in peace, tragedy and comedy march side by side.

An auction sale was being held at the head of Halifax Street. A mahogany wardrobe was offered for sale. The bidding went on until finally the auctioneer went into his chant: "Going — going — going once — going twice" — just then a shell came over, a fragment shattering the wardrobe — and "gone," he shouted as he took to his heels — "gone to General Grant!"

We are told that an army moves on its stomach, and when it doesn't move the citizens share the problems. During the Siege everything was in short supply, and generally made out of something else. Coffee was made out of parched sweet potatoes, sorghum, the "long sweetening," doubled for sugar, tea was made out of blackberry leaves, salt was boiled from planks in the smokehouse floor, and goodness knows what was in Confederate whiskey. The soldiers said it would make a nun swear!

Clothes came out of curtains, and petticoats led a double life. When a flag was wanted at Poplar Lawn after it was turned into a hospital, a yellow satin dress was flung out to the breeze, and when a safe deposit was needed a lady sewed her silver in her red flannel petticoat!

And, of course, anybody's clothes were for everybody. A story was told by one of the great ladies of Petersburg. She had the honor of calling on General Lee at his headquarters up on High Street.

She was then a very little girl, in her best clothes (also her brother's), including a hand-me-down jacket. She was full of importance as she sallied forth with her basket on her arm.

"Tell us," said a friend, "about the time you took the delicacy to General Lee."

"Delicacy?" the story teller laughed merrily, "It was some dried apples!"

23

It was the best the family had to offer, however, so, of course, it went to Marse Robert.

The young lady came home full of tears and disappointment, as she sobbed out the story of her visit: "General Lee 'frought' me was a boy!"

Another story of food for the General is told of Chelsea, an old home on Franklin Street.

General Lee came to dinner. It was Sunday and there was chicken! Mrs. Pryor, the hostess, noticed that the General ate his potatoes and corn bread, but carefully pushed the chicken to the side of his plate.

"General," she said, "you are not eating your chicken."

He replied that a member of his staff was sick — he was sure the chicken would tempt his appetite, so —

His hostess interrupted to say he could have some more chicken for the sick officer, then the General consented to eat his.

When Mrs. Pryor gave him the chicken carefully wrapped in a napkin, the General thanked her, promising he'd bring the napkin back next Sunday, and he did.

"Winter poured down its snows and sleets upon Lee's shelterless men in the trenches."

"Some of them," says Dr. White in his *Life of Lee,* "burrowed in the earth. Many of them shivered over the feeble fires burning along the lines. Scanty and thin were the garments of these heroes, most of them being clad in mere rags. Gaunt famine oppressed them every hour. One quarter of a pound of rancid bacon and a little meal was the daily ration."

After the fight at Hatcher's Run on the 5th of February, General Lee wrote: "Under these circumstances, heightened by assaults, and fire of the enemy, some of the men had been without meat for three days, and all were suffering from reduced rations and scanty clothing; exposed to battle, cold, hail, and sleet. The physical strength of the men must fail, if their courage survives."

They didn't have enough clothing, enough shoes, enough food — finally they were eating parched corn, taken from the horses' feed — they didn't have enough ammunition, enough blankets, enough oilcloth, enough anything. But their courage survived.

Meantime in the city they were striving "to make merriment of misery." They had "starvation parties," so-called for a very good reason. Dr. Claiborne says: "Ball followed ball, and the soldier met and danced with his lady love at night, and on the morrow danced the dance of death in the deadly trench on the line, and the comrade who reported his fate took his place on the following night in the festive hall, and often met the same fate on the following day."

The play must go on; and Petersburg played her part, supported mostly by corn bread and courage.

Dr. Claiborne tells many stories of the Siege. He could; it is a doctor's story. He had many difficulties with medical supplies, they were contraband of war. And he had small resources for trading. Tobacco, currency of the realm in Jamestown days, was again the medium of exchange. There was a minimum of cotton cloth for bargaining, but little else. These he exchanged for quinine, morphine, and chloroform.

One day he asked for a detail to guard the transportation of these precious supplies to a safe zone. Two soldiers from Georgia appeared for the duty. He directed them to the depot, and one asked if he could get some chewing tobacco from the commissary, "Go on," said the Doctor, "In twenty minutes you will probably have no mouth to put it in."

"In less time than that," Dr. Claiborne adds sorrowfully, "the man was brought back mortally wounded, a good part of his face carried away by a shell."

Some vital vignettes are given by the Doctor. "Lee, the peerless, passing along Washington Street on 'Traveller' toward some officer's quarters, near the lines in Blandford, riding along without courier or staff, as was his wont; of mien so dignified that no man could presume on familiarity, and yet so gracious a child might approach him."

"A. P. Hill, the *preux chevalier*, riding with easy grace, alert, as if looking for the enemy, and facing generally to the right, seeking, probably to inspect his lines where the weak point lay, and finally meeting his end charging alone upon Yankee pickets demanding their surrender. A. P. Hill, the intrepid leader for four years of the Light Division of the Army of Northern Virginia, and the only man upon whom both Lee and Jackson called as they fought their battles in their dying delirium, 'Tell A. P. Hill to prepare for action.'"

Another close-up of Marse Robert's boys — Captain McCabe says that on one of the last days of the war General Lee suddenly appeared in the field.

25

"It was touching to see the affection which lit up every dirty courageous face as he passed along the lines, amusing to hear the homely remarks indicative of their perfect confidence in his skill. 'I wonder what Marse Robert is after this rainy morning? Never you mind, his head is level and he knows, and that's enough.'" It was enough for them, enough for history. As has been said: "As far as one man could, General Lee did."

Perhaps this mighty spirit was nowhere better reflected than at Fort Gregg. The outlines of the old fort remain, Petersburg's Thermopolae. In this last desperate defense of the city, they did not quit as long as a man could hold a gun, and when they did, every man was a casualty.

Finally with the first of April came the battle of Five Forks; the last sigh of the Confederacy.

This was the end. "On Sunday night, April 2nd," reports Captain McCabe, "the lines of Petersburg and Richmond . . . were evacuated, and the Army of Northern Virginia, passed out in retreat. Thus were yielded at the last forty miles of entrenchments guarded by less than 40,000 men, yet held during ten months of ceaseless vigil and fevered famine with such grim tenacity as had made it hard for the brave of every nation to determine whether to accord their sorrowful admiration more to the stern prowess of the simple soldiers or to the matchless readiness of a leader who by the fervor of his genius developed from slender resources such an amazing power."

Early in the morning of April 3d, the Confederate troops were safely across the Appomattox.

At sunrise the Stars and Stripes floated over the Courthouse.

The Siege was over, and so was the war. On the ninth of April the army of "tattered uniforms and bright muskets" were at Appomattox Court House.

Captain McCabe says, "The bravest and the best . . . surrendered with their muskets in their hands (noblesse oblige!) at Appomattox."

He adds, all that was left was the "folded flag, the broken sword."

No, not quite all. There was left an enduring answer to the poet's query: "Oh why should the spirit of mortal be proud?"

And in Petersburg the old breastworks remain to this day. There century-old pines, rising from a brown carpet of pine needles, tell an eloquent story of the heroic defense of an old, well-loved city. The wind whispers in the pines, and the needles come sifting down — sifting and sighing over a Lost Cause.

26

CUCUMBER TREE — *Unusual in Virginia, the* MAGNOLIA ACUMINATA *shaded Sunday services at Violet Bank during the siege of Petersburg. General Lee joined his men in their religious observances. The top view is a summer scene. The bottom view reveals the great size and distinctive shape.*

MEMORIAL DAY

**I**N PETERSBURG the 30th of May is the 9th of June. No, we don't have a different calendar, but for Petersburg this is the day dyed with the blood of her sons. On June 9th, 1864, every man fit for military service was gone. The ones left were too old, too young, or too sick. The old men and boys went out to defend the city.

General Kautz and his cavalry were pounding down the Jerusalem Plank Road toward Petersburg.

At nine o'clock in the morning the great bell of the Courthouse clanged furiously. This was the signal to alert the residents. The bell rang out and from the homes and hospitals and the jail, poured every man able to fire a gun — if he could find a gun.

They followed Col. Fletcher H. Archer out to the edge of town, a little huddle of men — one hundred and twenty-five, where they took their positions and "stood to the breastworks like veterans."

They were joined by five or six men from a nearby battery with one gun — a small howitzer. When the sergeant was commanded to fire he said, "I have no shells, sir." And later when the decision to charge was made, the answer came, "We have no bayonets."

But they hung on. They hung on until they were being shot in the back while facing the enemy in the front.

They lost half a mile, but they gained half an hour. This saved the city.

Captain Edward Graham (a Petersburg boy) came thundering up Sycamore Street with his battery. He went into action on the Heights, opening fire on the Union troops advancing up the ravine. This stopped them, and Kautz hastily retreated.

A scant half hour, but never was time more dearly bought.

One hundred twenty-five men against 1300 Union troops. One hundred twenty-five went out, but before the day was over, more than half were killed, wounded or missing.

Dr. Douglas S. Freeman says it was "perhaps the unique battle of the entire war."

General Henry A. Wise, writing in 1864, reminds us of Churchill four score years later.

General Wise says: "Petersburg is to be and shall be defended on her outer walls, on her inner lines, at her corporation bounds, on every street and around every temple of God and altar of man, in every heart, until the blood of that heart is spilt."

And so on the 9th of June — every 9th of June since 1864 — we gather our posies and our pride and march again to Blandford Cemetery. We fill our baskets with flowers from the garden to make a living flag on the graves of the veterans. We strip the hollyhocks of their red silk blossoms for the field of the flag, then cross it with larkspur, starred with white feverfew — the battle flag of the Confederacy.

And here to Blandford Cemetery on a June day soon after the war came the wife of a Union officer, General John Logan. She and a party of friends had come to Virginia to visit the battlefields.

This is the story.

"Miss Lillie," we asked one of Petersburg's great ladies of yesterday, "just where did the idea of Memorial Day begin?"

"It began right here in Petersburg — in a woman's heart."

Miss Lillie folded her hands in her black silk lap, and her eyes were soft under the gray "crimps" of her hair — "It began in a woman's heart, long, long ago."

"You see," she went on, "it was the custom of the ladies of the Memorial Association to decorate the graves of the soldiers. Well, one day — in 1866 it was — they were at Blandford with their flags and flowers when a hack drove up . . . "

"A 'hack'?"

"Oh, you know, one of those old black closed carriages with the fringe . . . "

"On top, and all turning green? And a horse outside and horsey smelling inside . . . "

Miss Lillie laughed. "I see you remember. Well, Mrs. Logan was in the hack, and when she saw the flags fluttering over the hillside, she asked John (John Dixie was the Negro driver) what the ladies were doing. When John told her they were decorating the 'sojers', Mrs. Logan said she would

CONFEDERATE MEMORIAL — *Unlike counterparts throughout the South, this stone sentinel in Blandford Cemetery stands guard over the graves of 30,000 Confederates. Rising high on the horizon, this memorial symbolizes the position given to the holocaust brought to Petersburg by the Civil War.*

get out and speak to the ladies. But a member of the party demurred — he thought the Southern ladies might not welcome another Yankee invasion — however, Mrs. Logan only smiled as she stepped out of the carriage and said: 'A lady is always a lady, no matter where you find her!' "

"Good," we burst out enthusiastically, "and did the Blue and the Gray mix all right?"

"Of course — they liked each other entirely — and Mrs. Logan and Mrs. Joynes, head of the association, became lifelong friends. And Mrs. Logan was so impressed with the idea of a memorial day that she persuaded the General (who was a member of Congress) to work for a National Memorial Day."

"Oh — and didn't the G.A.R. take it up?"

"Yes, and they designated the 30th of May to honor their fallen comrades. So ever since 1868 there has been a National Memorial Day." Miss Lillie's eyes were soft as she looked across to the faraway hills, hearing, perhaps, the throb of distant drums.

As we gather in Blandford Churchyard on the 9th of June, which we've done for nearly a century, the memorial service ends with the bugler playing taps. A silver sound in the magnolia-scented dusk — a silver thread binding the past to the present.

THE BATTLE OF THE CRATER

IT HAS BEEN SAID that the Battle of the Crater is the most spectacular event in our history. Certainly it is one of the most tragic. People from all over the world have come to see this "dark and bloody" ground, where in a short and terrific battle, nearly six thousand men were killed and wounded.

It was the night of July 29-30, 1864. A hot, sultry night. Suddenly a terrific explosion tore through the silence, sending up a giant cloud of smoke, mushrooming to the sky. It descended, bearing in the flames the bodies of men. It slashed a great crater in the earth, immediately filled with screaming, dying men.

This, the tragedy of the Crater, was the end of a mighty effort by the Union to take Petersburg, and end the War between the States.

All through the spring of 1864, the scene of the war had steadily shifted to the James River area of Richmond, the Confederacy's capital as the objective.

The Confederates had their back to the wall — and Petersburg was the wall. When Petersburg fell, the way would be open to Richmond and the end of the war.

For this purpose General Grant had assembled an army of 40,000 men. He took his stand, and took his seat.

It began to look as if it would take all summer, when Lt. Col. Henry Pleasants, a young mining engineer of the 48th Pennsylvania Regiment, made a suggestion which he hoped would cause the fall of Petersburg and the end of the war. He planned to tunnel under the Confederate works and blow them up. So the Yankees began to dig. This was a war of nerves. The Confederates could hear them digging, but failed to locate the tunnel.

At last it was finished — a tunnel over 500 feet long, mined with four tons of black powder.

All was ready. The fuse was sparked. It was a hot, breathless night. The men, the very air itself, waited . . . and waited. But no explosion came.

THE CRATER — *Shaded and quiet, little evidence remains at the scene of the Union explosion on July 30, 1864, which threw Confederates and earth 200 feet in the air and left a crater 30 feet deep.*

Then occurred one of those high points in human behavior which swells the heart with pride, and bows it with humility. Two Pennsylvania miners, Lieutenant Douty and Sergeant Reese, volunteered to crawl back in the tunnel and relight the fuse!

Very appropriately, Pennsylvania has erected an imposing monument in memory of her heroic sons. But the names of Douty and Reese were already listed with the immortals.

Finally, in the gray dawn the explosion came. "Just at sunrise," an eyewitness wrote, "I looked to the front and saw a huge column of dirt, dust, smoke and flame — 200 feet high which on reaching its point curled over like a plume and came down with a dull thud to earth. While in the air I could see in the column of fire and smoke the bodies of men, arms, and legs, pieces of timber and a gun carriage."

If this belching fire and smoke was a volcano, the crater it tore in the earth was an inferno. The Union troops charged. But the first men disappeared in this terrible maw — it swallowed them up — literally the jaws of death. The men floundered, fell and died. More came on but could not get out of the Crater, then the order came: "Throw in the dead men." This they did. On came another charge, until there were sixteen Standards quivering there.

In the carnage, and confusion, and delay, the Confederates rallied. Their cannon found the range and shells poured on the Crater. A spectacular charge, led by General William Mahone, followed, and the terrible battle of the Crater was over.

The Yankee plan to open the way to Richmond, by taking the cemetery of old Blandford Church, had failed. The cemetery took them.

The ghastly experiment had cost the Union 4,000 killed and wounded, and the Confederacy 1,500.

The Petersburg Battlefield Park, climaxed by the Crater, tells a vivid story. The pages of history unfold. The events of yesterday are as sharp, and as stark, as though caught by a candid camera.

Today, pointed cedars stab the sky; tall pines wave solemn plumes, and pine needles, gently sifting down, have woven a silken shroud for the giant grave of the Crater.

Here men have died; here heroism lives.

BLANDFORD CHURCH

HIS STURDY OLD CHURCH, brick mellowed by the suns and storms of two hundred years, stands guard over the graves of the soldiers of six wars. Here are the known, the unknown, British, American, those who wore the blue, and 30,000 who wore the gray.

Blandford is a soldiers' saga.

The old "Brick Church" as it was called, was built in 1734-1737. In 1781, the British General, William Phillips, of Revolutionary fame was buried here.

In the spring of that year, Benedict Arnold, turned traitor, came up the James River, and was joined by General Phillips, who landed at City Point and marched on Petersburg.

Phillips took possession, and established headquarters at "East Hill," home of the Bolling family at Bollingbrook.

Lafayette, called by the British in derision, "the boy" — he was only twenty-four — took his position on the heights on the north side of the Appomattox, and began to shell the city.

Lafayette knew that Phillips was at Bollingbrook, but did not know that the General was ill.

A shell hit the house, and Phillips is said to have moaned: "Why won't the boy let me die in peace?"

A Negro servant, old Molly (so the story goes) was carrying a tray of food to the house, and was struck by a shell and killed.

A few hours later, General Phillips died and was buried in Blandford Cemetery. It is said that to prevent identification of the General's grave, he was buried first, and then Molly, in the same grave.

In a corner of the old churchyard, this spot cradled in ivy, and starred with the blue of periwinkle, has been kept sacred to the memory of General William Phillips.

The Daughters of the American Revolution have erected a marker to William Phillips, described by Thomas Jefferson as "the proudest man of the proudest nation on earth."

Moving on through the saga, we come to the War of 1812.

A company of Petersburg volunteers, under Captain Richard McRae, acquitted themselves so well in Canada, that on their return President Madison personally thanked them, and because of the little ornament in their caps, he dubbed Petersburg "The Cockade City" of the Union.

Oddly enough Petersburg is the setting for the last act of two historical sequences, the Revolution, ending at Yorktown, and the final scene of the Confederacy, at Appomattox.

Petersburg breathes drama.

1608 — Enter John Smith.

1645-46 — Fort Henry is erected to protect the "frontier," evolving into a trading station with the Indians — trading a life for a life.

1864-65 — The Siege — the Crater — Five Forks, the last sigh of the Confederacy — final curtain, Appomattox.

Blandford Churchyard has weathered many battles, but in 1864 it *was* the battle — the Crater. Cemetery Ridge, as it was called, was the Union objective, occupied by the Confederate troops.

One of the stories that has come down to us is of a soldier who settled himself on a large, flat tombstone for a long night's sleep. It came near to being his last. In fact, he told his family afterward, he thought it *was* his last. The "last trump," however, was not Gabriel's but the Yankees'. They had exploded the Crater mine.

He awakened to find he was buried, covered with mud and stones. He mused on his fate, tentatively moved one foot — the other. Then came the glorious discovery — he was buried but not dead! He dug his way through the debris, pulled himself up on the tombstone, and stood erect — muddy, but unbowed!

Blandford is our Stoke Poges. The stories told by the old stones are here for all to read; stories of sacrifice, of heroism and humility. And though we are without benefit of Thomas Gray, we do have an elegy by an anonymous poet. Tradition credits the Irish comedian, Tyrone Power, ancestor of the late popular movie actor. In 1841, when the old Church was in disuse,

39

battered by man and bruised by nature, these lines were found pencilled
on the wall:

Thou art crumbling to the dust, old pile,
    Thou art hastening to thy fall,
And round thee in thy loneliness
    Clings the ivy to the wall.
The worshippers are scattered now
    Who knelt before thy shrine,
And silence reigns where anthems rose
    In days of "Auld Lang Syne."

And sadly sighs the wandering wind
    Where oft in years gone by,
Prayers rose from many hearts to Him,
    The Highest of the High;
The tramp of many a busy foot
    That sought thy aisles is o'er,
And many a weary heart around
    Is still for evermore.

How doth ambition's hope take wing,
    How droops the spirit now!
We hear the distant city's din,
    The dead are mute below.
The sun that shone upon their paths
    Now gilds their lonely graves;
The zephyr which once fanned their brows
    The grass above them waves.

Oh! could we call the many back
    Who've gathered here in vain —
Who've careless roved where we do now,
    Who'll never meet again;
How would our very souls be stirred,
    To meet the earnest gaze
Of the tender and the beautiful
    The lights of other days.

BLANDFORD CHURCH — *Erected between 1734 and 1737 and known originally as the Brick Church on Well's Hill, this church is now a Confederate Memorial Chapel. The beautiful cemetery — scene of Revolutionary and Civil War battles — contains graves of famous and unknown, soldiers and civilians.*

Many stories cluster around the old cemetery. On one tomb the inscription reads:

HONOR WAS HIS ONLY VICE

Francis Antomatti, a gentleman and a Corsican, loved a beautiful maid, Farnerina. She was described in the language of the day as having "alabaster skin," and "hair black as a raven's wing."

The romance did not prosper. Antomatti, in the humility of love, perhaps, felt himself unworthy of his inamorata. One evening, just at sunset, he climbed to the gallery of the Church, and took his last look across the hills at the home of his beloved. He slashed his throat and fell to the floor below, where his body was discovered next morning.

Over his tomb the hemlocks wave solemn plumes. But underneath the fragrant carpet of tiny needles, the worn inscription can still be read:

FRANCIS ANTOMATTI

Died July 31, 1844

HONOR WAS HIS ONLY VICE

The old Church is restored now, and serves as a Confederate Memorial Chapel. Visitors from all over the world have come to sightsee, and, perhaps, remained to pray.

The Tiffany windows, reflecting in lambent glass, the life of the Apostles, are memorials to the Confederate States. If the visitor only reads the inscription on the Alabama window — "Brave men may die — Right has no death — Truth shall never pass away" — the silent men in the churchyard will have found a voice.

OUR FIRST FIRST LADY

AS WE APPROACH Jamestown from the old road, the James River, two figures greet us. One is Captain John Smith, whose courage saved Virginia; the other is Pocahontas, whose courage saved him. The lengthened shadow of these two reaches to the Pacific Ocean — that fabled sea that Smith set out to find, when he was captured by the Indians.

This is the story, related by the doughty Captain himself.

Smith and a few other "venturers" had gone up the Chickahominy River to find the Pacific — and/or some much-needed bushels of corn.

They advanced until they could go no further and Smith went ashore, leaving the men to guard the barge.

The men were killed, and a band of screaming Indians surrounded Smith. He bound his Indian guide to his side with his garter, using him for a shield. Even Smith's ingenuity and courage could not prevent his capture, however, and finally he is led to the great "werowance," the Emperor Powhatan.

The Chief, clad in a rich robe of raccoon skins was seated in his arbor-like wigwam, surrounded by one hundred bowman, beautiful girls, and favored wives.

The inscrutable bronze face of Powhatan looked down on the proceedings in dreadful silence. Finally, a huge stone is brought in and Smith is dragged to it. "Then," he says, "a big Indian raised his club to beat out my brains, when God's mercy sent to my succor one of his angels."

The "angel," a girl of twelve or thirteen, is "the King's dearest daughter — I 'had taken note of her,' Smith says, 'for her extreme grace and come-liness' . . . She ran and clasped my head and held me close to her heart. With tears streaming down she holds me close to her bosom, and murmurs pitifully that I be spared."

Powhatan leans on his hand — holds out his big red arm, he with the club falls back, and (says Smith) "I am saved."

POCAHONTAS' BASIN — *Legends state that Powhatan gave his daughter, Pocahontas, lands in the vicinity of Petersburg as a marriage gift. This basin, once beside the Appomattox River, the legends continue, was used by the Indian princess. One of the most photographed of the city's scenes, it is now located in Poplar Lawn.*

The legend of Pocahontas runs through the early history of the colony like a golden thread. It shines out through the dark days of desperation and starvation, when she came to the relief of the half-crazed people. And but for her, we should not have celebrated more than three centuries of "America," which, says an early writer "the new fashion is to call Virginia."

On a spring day in 1607, a hundred hardy souls, believing that "God would not have this fine country unplanted by Englishmen," arrived at Jamestown.

The three tiny ships folded their wings, after long ship-weary months on the Atlantic. Beckoning pines welcomed Smith and the band of stalwarts to the willow-green shore. The woods were glowing with redbud, and sweet with the mystery of May. No wonder the weary travellers felt that "Heaven and earth never agreed better to frame a place for man's habitation."

And Master Drayton rhapsodizes: They are come

> To get the pearl and gold,
> And ours to hold
> Virginia,
> Earth's only paradise.

But hidden in this paradise were the creeping evils of savagery, ignorance, treachery, illness, and starvation.

Into this dark picture comes Pocahontas.

Let Anas Todkill, one of the very early settlers, describe her. In "My Lady Pokahontas," he says, "the maid came toward us, stepping with a pretty and proud gait, like a fawn. Her hair was black and straight, but scarce seen for the white plume in it . . . She comes putting down each little foot, covered with bead moccasins, and smiling out of black eyes."

Pocahontas, "the playful one" as she was called, walked right into the hearts of Virginians — and has been there ever since.

We, in Petersburg, "on the pleasant river of Appomatuck," cherish the memory of Virginia's first first lady. We have named two towns for her — Pocahontas and Matoaca — this last her very private Indian name, known only to her closest friends.

Down by the river, near Pocahontas, one of our oldest inhabitants re-told the story handed down from his forefathers. Tradition, that minstrelsy of the heart, sings through the years. "Yes, ma'am," said the aged Negro in answer to our queries, "this is where the pappy of Pocahontas tribed."

Her pappy, Powhatan, and Uncle Opechancanough "tribed" all through this section. Perhaps the Princess Pocahontas roamed the gentle hills around us. In fact, that is the only criticism we have heard of our laughing girl. A grande dame — one of the great ladies of yesterday — said she was proud of her heritage (she was descended from Pocahontas) — "But — I really don't approve of the way she ran about the woods *unchaperoned!*"

Unchaperoned, or not, we believe she visited the site of our Pocahontas town. There we found the old hewed-out granite stone, which we call the Pocahontas Basin. We have given this a place of honor in Poplar Lawn. Perhaps the playful Pocahontas dipped her raven hair in this basin. Certain it is that half of the soldiers at Fort Lee have used it as a background for snapshots to send back home.

Pocahontas played many parts in Jamestown. She came as a lady bountiful. Anas Todkill described her — "in a robe of bird's feathers — black eyes, and hair of the same color with never a curl in it, in which drooped a plume of white feathers, her badge of princess." Following her, says Anas, " a wild train of attendants with full baskets weigh down the backs of her dusky people."

The romance of Pocahontas and John Smith has had many interpretations. Our friend Todkill says: "She and Smith much affected each other," but " it was not a time for dalliance when men were muttering and falling into mutiny."

"Certes" (excuse us, Master Todkill), keeping the colony from complete destruction, occupied Smith's entire attention.

Jamestown was swept now with a more insidious disease than the mosquito-borne malaria — the gold fever. "There was no thought but to dig gold, wash gold, refine gold, load gold. They fraught their drunken ship with their gilded dirt."

It was found in London to be what the wise ones knew in Virginia — worthless.

The result of the gold fever was devastating. Planting had been neglected; there was no corn. Smith's determination saved them. He issued his iron dictum: "He that will not work shall not eat." One of the early writers says: "Smith was to tend and plant the ground purchased by his own courage."

Added to Smith's courage was the kindness of Pocahontas. Many times her good offices saved the colonists. On one of the Captain's foraging expeditions, she slipped through the "fearsome woods" at night to warn him that Powhatan planned to massacre them all.

When Smith wanted to give her some trinkets to show his gratitude, she did not dare take them; she said that Powhatan would kill her.

At last came the accident that sent the Captain back to England. He was returning from a foraging expedition in a small boat when there was an explosion of gunpowder. Smith was frightfully burned. Half crazed, he jumped into the water. The result of this accident was so serious that he returned to England for treatment.

Anas Todkill bade him farewell: "What can I say of him we thus lost, save that truth and justice were his guides; that he hated sloth and baseness worse than danger and death; that he would send his men nowhere that he would not lead himself; that he loved action more than words and hated falsehood more than death; whose adventures were our lives, and whose loss was our deaths."

Anas returned to the dreary palisade. He looked around for the Lady Pocahontas. She is not here, "but is gone away to her York woods, weeping, they say."

The situation at Jamestown grew steadily worse, until finally there was no corn. It was the Starving Time. Says Todkill, "Man died of famine looking with dumb amaze each in the others eyes. At last all was eaten, hogs, sheep, and horses. Acorns, walnuts, berries and a few fish . . . we did eat the skin of horses and at last one another . . . One did kill his wife and had eat part of her ere we knew it, for which we burned him, as he well deserved . . ."

At last there were left only sixty souls — all that remained of the once flourishing colony.

And then, one day: A sail! A sail!

"Blessed be God," says Anas, "for there was a sail coming up the river; nay, two white sails against the fringe of woods."

"The foremost was the cedar ship, built by brave Admiral Somers in the Bermuda Islands, whereon the *Sea-Venture* has been shipwrecked the year before. This was the *Deliverance,* for which deliverance God be thanked."

A dreary picture met the visitors, Sir Thomas Somers and the Lieutenant Governor, Sir Thomas Gates. The cabins were nearly gone for firewood, and the palisades half torn down. The gates swung on broken hinges, and the Fort platform scarce held up the cannon.

The colonists crowded forward with cries of "Bread, bread" — and in the next breath, "England, England!"

Somers promises to take them back. Says Todkill: "They would have burned the cursed place that they could never return to it . . . We buried the cannon at the gate of the Fort — a guard is posted in the palisades and hurries the poor people aboard. The drum rolls for the signal and all are shipped . . ." The Admiral comes aboard. A salute is fired — the ships move . . . Farewell to Jamestown!

"But," says our chronicler, "said I not that God would not have this land of Virginia fall back to heathenesse?"

The ships stop at Mulberry Isle. Here at dawn, came a swift barge shooting up the river, flying the English pennant.

Lord De la Warr is coming with more ships and more Englishmen. He issues orders to go back to Jamestown and await him — this they did.

Lord De la Warr comes with flags flying, and lands on shore — he prays for "a season," glad at heart that he comes in time to save Virginia. "The drums roll, the Church is open for service, and all is joy in the Virginia plantation, which was dead and is alive again."

Time, as time will, flows on. It is now the "falling-of-the-leaf." October has trailed her rainbow scarf across the Virginia hills, and spread a royal carpet through the woods. Down this russet pathway comes the Princess Pocahontas. With her is an Englishman, "an honest gentleman of good behavior," Master John Rolfe.

He had lost his wife and infant daughter on the ill-fated *Sea Venture,* wrecked on the Bermudas. These "devil's isles" were thought by seamen to be bewitched. Many were the tales that came from these mysterious shores — not the least *The Tempest,* by one William Shakespeare.

John Rolfe was a man of parts, and high in the councils of the colony. But he was a sad and lonely man.

Pocahontas, says our friend Anas, "was young and mirthful, and affected company, and others affected her." Particularly Master Rolfe. Anas reports: ". . . soon I saw that this so great wound in the heart of Master Rolfe was well-nigh healed, for he had begun to love my little Lady Pocahontas."

And (saith Master Rolfe), "This gracious creature hath made a mighty war in my meditations."

He thinks he will square things with his conscience by converting Pocahontas — (to convert them is to love them) so he decides to marry the gracious creature, for the glory of God and the good of his people.

The "bruit" has come that Smith is dead, and says Anas, what better can she do "than bethink her that one loves her that still liveth and will cherish her."

For some months Pocahontas has been held as a hostage in Jamestown. Through a ruse she was captured and held prisoner, in order to force Powhatan to release some Englishmen and arms.

Pocahontas has been well treated and she likes the English. She has adopted their religion and their ruffs. She is carefully dressed, and Anas says, "spends much time on her hair at the back of her head, seeking to make it curl, and put it in a cushion." (*Editor's note:* Every woman, before and since Pocahontas, who falls in love, changes the style of her hair!) "On her feet [Anas again] were Spanish shoes of green morocco, with high red heels, with clocked stockings on the ankles. Her round arms were ever naked, with coral bracelets on her wrists, and as she moved the slim figure of the maid was like a willow-tree, such as groweth on Virginia rivers."

'Powhatan, when he learned that Pocahontas had been taken prisoner by the English "is bitter offendeth."

Messages go to him from Sir Thomas Dale, saying that Pocahontas will be sent back when the captive Englishmen, and their muskets, are returned.

Nothing comes of these overtures, however, so Sir Thomas decides that he will go to Powhatan. He takes a picked band of men, including John Rolfe. And also with him is the Lady Pocahontas.

Powhatan was not at Werowocomoco to receive him, but a great multitude of Indians were, who welcomed them with a shower of arrows.

The English push on to Machot, Opechancanough's capital city. John Rolfe is sent as a messenger to treat with the Indian Chief, but the Chief would not parley with the English.

Sir Thomas concludes that he is being trifled with, and is about to give orders to lay waste all houses, when suddenly "something stops all." The Lady Pocahontas in a brave gown, and looking very proud, had come ashore with the rest. Then she said: "If my father loved me he would not value me less than old swords, pieces, or axes; so I will still dwell with the Englishmen, who love me."

The matter is settled — the men and pieces shall be brought to the English — Sir Thomas will not fulfill his intent to destroy the heathen — they will be friends, since one of his gentlemen will wed with their princess.

The ship is loaded with corn — the prisoners are returned — Pocahontas bids goodbye to her brother, Nantaquaus, and tells him to come to the wedding. Peace is made. The ship sails down the York River and returns to Jamestown. Once more this Indian maid was the guardian angel of the white and red people in this land of Virginia.

And so Rolfe married the Princess. It is 1616 — a sweet spring day, April is in attendance, dressed in satin green, and through the woods there floats a veil of dogwood lace.

The bell rings out from the old church tower. Inside there is a study in contrasts. Virginians, old and new, have come to see the Indian princess wed the "white face." Jerkins and gold-laced doublets are pressed against bare red shoulders. Brave English wigs are topped by the colorful, swaying feathers of the Indians.

Pocahontas, in bridal white, is flanked by the bronze figures of her two favorite brothers.

They are met at the old canoe-like font by John Rolfe. Here the Reverend Richard Buck performed the ceremony, to the accompaniment of murmuring pines from the open windows, and the sweet incense of the old cedar pews.

John and Madame Rolfe went to live at Varina on the James. Here he found the gold which had proved so elusive to the colonists: The Golden Weed! He improved and perfected a strain of tobacco which was not only a money-crop, but money itself, in the early days of the colony. John Rolfe was the first man to turn tobacco into big money. Three hundred years later, Virginia is still puffing away at Master Rolfe's ideas.

After a peaceful sojourn at Varina, where her little son, Thomas, is born, Madame Rolfe decides that she wants to go abroad.

Says Master Todkill: "She could not well endure the society of her own nation. The true affection she constantly bore her husband was much — he, on the other hand, underwent great torment and pain out of his violent passion and tender solicitude for her."

And so they sailed for England. Pocahontas took with her several attendants — among them Tomocomo, who was provided with a long stick, on which he was to make a notch for every Englishman he saw. The stick just wasn't long enough. Tomocomo said "his arithmetic failed him"; he gave up.

In due course Pocahontas meets John Smith. She is much affected when she sees him. She saluted him modestly, but turned around and "obscured her face as not seeming well contented." She cannot understand the false report of his death, but she talks to him, and claims friendship and kinship, since Powhatan had adopted the Captain into the tribe.

But Smith was a politician as well as a soldier. He knew the jealousy of the court, and realized that his place was no longer by the side of his little princess. The doughty Captain not only had the courage to advance, but the greater courage to retreat. He bowed out of the picture. As a farewell gesture, however, he writes a letter to the Queen, begging her indulgence on behalf of Pocahontas. Surely she deserved consideration, for said Smith, she "next under God, was still the instrument to preserve the colony, free from death, from famine, and utter confusion."

Pocahontas was received at court with much pomp and ceremony, and the comment was made that "she carrieth herself as the daughter of a king."

At last, in 1617, Pocahontas decides to return to Virginia. She goes to Gravesend to embark. It is a raw March day. She is taken ill, and dies without seeing again the sunlit pines of Virginia.

She was buried in St. George's Church, Gravesend, England. The inscription reads: "A Virginia Gentlewoman, Wife to Mr. Rolfe."

Pocahontas, wife to Mr. Rolfe, and first lady of Virginia.

CENTRE HILL

❀

O N AN APRIL DAY in 1865, two figures stood on the wide portico of Centre Hill Mansion. General G. I. Hartsuff, the Union commander, is talking to Abraham Lincoln. The General has been using the house for his headquarters. When the question of rent is brought up, President Lincoln remarked that he thought "our batteries have made rent enough already." The "rent" can still be seen in the gouged-out corner of the wall.

The old house has lived through war and peace since 1823. It is a frank expression of nineteenth-century elegance. Huge marble dogs flank the imposing entrance, guarding the past. Under the tall columns, white against the background of mellow brick, have passed the great and near-great for more than a century.

One visitor, entering the wide hall with beautiful hand carving flung lavishly around the doors, exclaimed, "My goodness, has Williamsburg seen this?" Of course, Centre Hill is not historically old enough for Williamsburg, but the serene beauty of the mansion is ageless.

The high-ceilinged rooms are imposing — sweeping lines, with elaborate cornices and centre-pieces, which we are told is a lost art. These frothy decorations look like the apotheosis of the old-fashioned wedding cake. Festooned over the doors is a delicate, hand-carved motif, like ball fringe, that drips down the sides.

The old house speaks with many voices. The first of these was the builder of the house, Colonel Robert Bolling, great-grandson of the emigrant. Robert Bolling, the emigrant, was Mr. Petersburg, in person.

He was a man of parts, not lacking in imagination. The story is told of an early encounter of his with an Indian chief. The Indian had had a dream. And an Indian's dream absolutely prophesied things to come. You could no more argue with it than you could with a tomahawk; it was final. The Indian told Robert Bolling that he had a dream. And when Robert Bolling inquired further, the Indian said: "I dreamed that you gave me your horse."

This was a nightmare for Mr. Bolling, but he bowed to the inevitable, confirming the Indian custom, and handed over his favorite mount.

But it wasn't easy. We are told that we are such stuff as dreams are made on, and that applies to Petersburg.

The next time the Chief and Robert Bolling met, he told the Indian about *his* dream — he dreamed that the Indian had given him all the land that they could see, stretching away from the river.

Of course, the Indian code prevailed, and Robert Bolling became Petersburg's first realtor, in the best sense of the word. He and his descendants did much for the development of the city.

In other days other Bollings built their mansions, East Hill, West Hill, and, most impressive of all, Centre Hill.

The old house has played many parts. From under the willow-oaks that fringe the red brick with green, the Petersburg Volunteers departed to fight the British in 1812.

And a brave sight they must have been in their colorful uniforms, black crossed with white bands, and gold buttons, red-topped tasseled boots, and a wide-brimmed hat with a red band, with red and black feathers held in place by a cockade of ribbon.

They returned with a distinguished record for Canadian service, and an accolade from President Madison. When he reviewed the troops in Washington, he spoke of the decoration in their caps, and dubbed Petersburg, "The Cockade City of the Union."

Perhaps the most eloquent voices of Centre Hill are the flags. As we enter we see a large Confederate flag, called the Jackson Flag because it was used to cover the body of Stonewall Jackson.

This was the flag that flew over the Courthouse and was hauled down April 3, 1865, when the Yankees took the city. The Union General, Ralph Eley, carried it away. Many years later it was returned to Petersburg by his grandson.

Nearby is another eloquent flag. It looks as if it had been buried and dug up. And so it has. It was made by the ladies of Petersburg, and presented to the City Guards. To prevent its capture it was buried near Norfolk. Twenty years later it was unearthed and brought back to Petersburg. The old fabric is tattered and torn, but the inspiration of Virginia still gleams in the gold letters: "Sic Semper Tyrannis."

The A. P. Hill Confederate Veterans banner is carefully preserved in a glass case. It bears the date 1887. The brave old colors have stood up.

Another voice — a poignant one — is the old yellow flag which flew over the improvised hospital on Poplar Lawn. The call went out for something yellow to indicate the hospital, and soon there floated from the tallest Sycamore tree, Miss Mary Eccles's yellow satin dress!

Centre Hill is a series of symbols, which is perhaps what a museum is — a point of departure for a journey into the past.

There are guns, swords, shells, bullets — two that met head-on, and are fused together. Confederate money, described in the poet's fancy:

> Representing nothing on God's earth now,
> And naught in the waters below it —
> As the pledge of a nation that's dead and gone —
> Keep it, dear friend, and show it.

In the cases around the wall: Confederate uniforms, gray as ashes, but glowing with the red of the gallant sash, glinting with golden fringe.

A Testament, torn with a bullet — it saved a soldier's life at the Battle of the Crater. And one of the saddest symbols of all: a carpet bag.

From the make-do period of the South's history is a newspaper from Vicksburg, Mississippi, printed on wall paper.

Another newspaper called *Grant's Petersburg Progress,* was printed when the Union army took the city.

Under the head: "FASHIONABLE ARRIVALS — April 3d., Gen. Grant and staff and the Army of the Potomac Generally."

Then this item: "A five cent piece and a copper penny were found in Petersburg Courthouse this morning, supposed to be all the available specie in the City."

Another paragraph, headed: "THE SILENT DEPARTURE. The Confederates went out of the city in the greatest silence; The Union Army came in with general hurrahing and banners flying."

Then a human interest story: "In speaking of the curious anticks of our shells in flying about here and there, and their often striking, a creditable colored woman said in our hearing this morning she 'really believed our shells had men in them!'"

CENTRE HILL MANSION – *The great house, completed in 1823 by Colonel Robert Bolling, descendant of Pocahontas, has been the setting of social and military activity. It is now a museum.*

Under the caption: "AUCTION SALES: To be sold cheap 'if not badly sold already' the ineligible and worthless property known as the Southern Confederacy. For particulars apply, Jefferson Davis, Richmond, Va."

Some years later, another invasion of Yankees took place in Petersburg. The occasion was the unveiling of the imposing monument that Massachusetts erected to her gallant sons. On the wall of Centre Hill is an account of the dedication in November, 1911. It was a gala day. The northern delegation surrendered to southern hospitality, and the Blue and the Gray marched to the same drums.

Someone has written:

> Brave minds at war, are secret friends,
> Their generous discord with the battle ends,
> In peace, they wonder whence discussion rose
> And ask how souls so like could e'er be foes.

One of the delegation, Colonel James Anderson, affectionately known as "Jim Anderson," personally conquered the city, and was made an honorary member of the A. P. Hill Camp, Confederate Veterans.

For many years, Jim Anderson never failed to appear on General Lee's birthday for the annual dinner. His was the one blue coat among the gray. It was a colorful picture; gray heads, silver in the candle light, red roses marching down the white damask table cloth — the Confederate colors.

Jim Anderson reciprocated our hospitality by inviting the whole camp to come to Springfield, Massachusetts, as guests of the city. They went, they saw, and it is rumored they conquered. They had a splendid time, were wined and dined — "treated royally," they reported on their return.

Many were the gab-fests of the old Vets. One of them told us about it. He was talking to a Union Veteran with a deep scar on forehead, who had been near Petersburg during the War. The Petersburger asked him where he had been wounded, and the Union soldier said: "Below Petersburg, near Suffolk."

"Do you remember," said Johnny Reb, "an engagement near Suffolk, in the fall of '64 — just north of the city, at the crossroads?"

"I ought to," broke in the gentleman from Massachusetts, "that's where I was wounded . . ."

"I was in command of that 'piece,' and . . ."

"And," interrupted Blue Coat, "you are the very fellow who shot me!"

59

"I'm mighty sorry," said our Petersburg correspondent, "but," he added with a chuckle, "I'm glad I didn't hit you any harder!"

We were so fond of Jim Anderson that when the lady who had been his hostess for many visits, passed on to that land beyond wars, a mirror which the Colonel admired, was left to him.

It was a Victorian piece — a horn circling the glass, and it sat on the piano for years in an old Petersburg home.

It is now, we suppose, in Springfield, where its silver circle reflected the brave coats of blue.

Through the years, many distinguished guests have passed through the wide fan-lighted doorway to Centre Hill. The old mansion seems built to give a party — and party-giving is as much a part of Petersburg as old iron fences and magnolias.

On a May day in 1909, Centre Hill was the scene of one of the best parties we ever had — a reception to that genial President of the United States, William Howard Taft.

Mr. and Mrs. Charles Hall Davis were hosts to distinguished guests from the city, the state, and the nation.

The luncheon was an al fresco affair. The tables set out under the spreading trees were not glass-topped, but grass-topped. The grass was planted on wide hollowed-out tables and "got up" in six weeks to make a green velvet tablecloth.

It was a grand party. Everybody came, and an interesting program was published to commemorate the occasion, listing distinguished guests.

Another list of celebrities who had visited Petersburg before — three hundred years before — was added. Among these were Powahatan, Opechancanough, Pocahontas, John Smith, Sir Thomas Dale, and other early arrivals in Petersburg.

One of these, Pocahontas, has the distinction of being the grandmother, with appropriate "greats," of the Bolling family. Among the descendants is Mrs. Edith Bolling Wilson, widow of President Woodrow Wilson.

Mrs. Wilson, being captivated by the charm of Centre Hill, told a resident of Petersburg that it was long her ambition to come here and make her home at Centre Hill. Surely, no lovelier hostess could have graced the old mansion than this daughter of Virginia, and wife of one of Virginia's greatest sons.

Since 1950, Centre Hill has been a Confederate Museum, distinctive, interesting, unique. A committee of distinguished citizens, under the dedicated leadership of Mr. Walter T. McCandlish has gathered Petersburg memories into a museum.

These are the Trustees:

Centre Hill Mansion was once the heart of Petersburg; Centre Hill Museum will always be.

The old rooms throb with thoughts of yesterday, the cadence of marching feet, the "music of distant drums."

Welcome streams out from the house shadowed by the Golden-Rain tree. The wide, hospitable doors open to visitors from foreign lands and nearby states. Perhaps, as we climb the stone steps, we will hear the old watch dogs "bay deep-mouthed welcome as we draw near home."

GEORGE WASHINGTON TELLS ONE

E SHOULD NOT like you to think that in Petersburg we do nothing but fight. About a hundred years ago we didn't do much else. But then we were fighting in our own front yard, and stories of "de wah" are still going around.

Not long ago the young son of a friend came home from school with a bloody nose. He had been in a fight, and a good one. His mother's solicitous inquiries met with strangled sobs. Finally, he said, "Mother, didn't we win the war?"

"No, son, we didn't."

"Then why are we always talking about it?"

A point well taken. We do talk, we do fight, but next to a good fight we love a good party.

One of the best was a reception for George Washington in 1791. The President was making a tour of the South, and on a sunny April day he came to Petersburg. "He was met at Osborne's in Chesterfield County [says Pollock's Guide] by a detachment of the local cavalry and escorted into town. Elaborate preparations had been made for the suitable reception and entertainment of the distinguished guest. Triumphal arches were erected, and a grand public banquet was provided by order of the Common Hall. There was an address by the Mayor, Richard Bate, in which the 'All-wise Director of human events' was prayed to 'prolong the life of the Father of his Country . . .' "

We think this was the first time Washington was given this affectionate title.

According to Pollock's Guide, the President replied: "The Government of the United States, originating in the wisdom, supported by the virtue and having no other object than the happiness of the people, reposes not on the exertions of an individual; yet as far as integrity of intention may justify the belief, my agency in the administration will be constant to your favorable

THE COURT HOUSE — On June 9, 1864, the bells in the tower called out the militia, com-
posed mostly of old men and boys, to defend the city against its first Union attack. More than half
the 125 defenders were killed, wounded or captured in this — Petersburg's most heroic — effort.

operations, and my private wishes will always be preferred for the prosperity of Petersburg, and the particular welfare of its inhabitants."

After dinner at Armistead's Tavern, the President responded to many toasts in his honor, then they had a ball. The "fair sex" graced the occasion. General Washington had an eye for the ladies, and he counted them. He wrote in his diary that "60 or 70 ladies were present."

The visit was a great success, and then . . .

The President was asked when he would depart. We quote from his diary: "Having suffered very much by the dust of yesterday, and finding that parties of horse and a number of gentlemen were intending to attend me part of the way today, I caused their inquiries respecting the time of my setting out to be answered that I should endeavor to do so before 8 o'clock, but did it a little after five, by which means I avoided the inconvenience above mentioned."

With much shaking of heads, the old writers speak of "the illustrious backslider" in his only recorded departure from the truth.

Washington was first, last, and always an engineer. He was the engineer of our political destiny. As President of these United States he was adept in making a detour to avoid entanglements, and personally he wasn't going to get mixed up in any Virginia dust. So he threw some in our eyes to keep from getting it in his.

FANFARE AND FLOWERS

ETERSBURG LOVES COMPANY. When visitors come we put the big pot in the little one. One of these happy occasions was the reception to "the hero of two worlds." "The most notable event [says an early writer] was the visit of the Marquis de La Fayette," in 1824.

"In consequence of the conspicuous part he played in the history of the town during the Revolution, the Marquis had always been an object of affectionate interest to the inhabitants, and the reception accorded 'the hero of two worlds' was a perfect ovation. A troop on horses met him far beyond the corporation limits and his arrival was attended with all the 'pomp and circumstance' of a triumphal entry."

The evidence of happiness and prosperity which now met him from all sides must have contrasted vividly with the recollections of his former visit when he had overlooked the conquered town from behind the trunnions of his field pieces, planted on the heights of Chesterfield (Colonial Heights). Some such retrospect now engaged the veteran's mind for in replying to the Major's address of welcome he said: "I have in former times to lament the necessity in the course of military operations to disturb the repose of the good town of Petersburg while it had become a British headquarter, but in this very circumstance found new opportunities to witness her patriotism."

The Marquis and his entourage were banqueted in Niblo's Long Room, and afterward a ball was given for the distinguished French guest. This was in the Petersburg Theatre on Bollingbrook Street, built in 1818, and copied from Covent Garden in London.

"The pit," says an old record, "was floored over, the stage being hung with pink and roofed with blue, with a palace scene at the end. The top tier of boxes was filled with evergreens up to the roof and two lower tiers were reserved for the gentlemen, until Lafayette had made the circle of ladies in the rotunda, when he returned to his seat of honor and ten cotillion sets were danced at once."

66

The picture is a Fragonard come to life. Under the pink and blue hangings, there was the swish of taffeta, the cascade of lace, as the dancers bowed low in the stately measure of the minuet.

The next day, Lafayette was escorted to Poplar Lawn where four hundred school children strewed flowers in his path and sang this song:

> Welcome, welcome Lafayette,
> Thee we never can forget.
> Friend of man we love thee yet,
> Friendship — Liberty.
>
> Yes, we take thee by the hand,
> Welcome thee to our Southland.
> By thee we will ever stand,
> Firm and true to thee.

(A prelude to "Lafayette, we are here"?)

This tribute reduced the "grand old man" to tears. We are told that the noble Frenchman bade our town a last farewell. He was "A man" in the language of a local reporter, "than whom his superior does not dwell beneath the vaulted roof of heaven."

Entertainment is an integral part of Petersburg. It permeates the atmosphere like magnolias in June. In the old days, "put another place, Liza" was as much a part of daily living as "take two and butter them while they are hot."

Of course we love to talk, and the best talk seems to flow around the dining table.

George Washington wrote to William Fitzhugh that there was nowhere he (Gen. Washington) more enjoyed putting his legs under the mahogany than at Chatham, the Fitzhugh estate.

The "mahogany," or walnut, was a focal point of entertainment. The table was laid with care. An early English visitor to a James River plantation describes the setting . . . "each plate standing separate on its own little cloth."

Talk flourished at the table, cornbread and conversation just seem to go together in Virginia — and if you had "hawg jowl" and greens — but there, we've got around to banquets again!

In the early days banquets were held in Taverns or Ordinaries. These were many. Perhaps the most famous was the Golden Ball on Old Street, near Peter Jones's Trading Station. In the English tradition a golden ball adorned the sign. On the street in front there was a gong, which, promptly at noon, a mechanical Negro struck with an iron mace. This inspired a visitor from the country to remark that he thanked God that he had found one man in Petersburg who could mind his own business!

The gong was the voice of authority — dinner was ready. It was served with toddy, or small beer, and cost 2 shillings, 6 pence.

At the Golden Ball British officers were quartered during the Revolution. Another British officer, General O'Hara, stayed nearby in Dinwiddie County at the Long Or'nary. Later he was to go to Yorktown where he surrendered Cornwallis's sword to George Washington.

There was Powell's Tavern, a real 18th-century Coffee House run by Zip Roberts on Bollingbrook Street, and Dodson's on High Street, where Aaron Burr stayed with his charming daughter, Theodosia. Here (they say) she made cakes for her father whom she adored. She wrote: "I had rather not live than not to be the daughter of such a man."

Just before her eighteenth birthday in 1801, she married Joseph Alston, who became Governor of South Carolina. And (adds the chronicle) "the story of her tragic death is as romantic as sad."

Her death is shrouded in mystery. One story has it that she was on a ship captured by pirates.

The Southside Democrat of Petersburg, reported this story in 1856: "A sailor living near New Orleans sent for a minister. On his deathbed he confessed the murder of a lady on one of the ships they had captured. She begged for life, finding that of no avail she arose from her knees and said she would go out on the plank herself.

"The usual plunge in the deep announced this additional victim to the number already destroyed."

The account continues: "This could have been no other than Theodosia, wife of Governor Alston . . . It is probable that such was the end of the affectionate daughter of Aaron Burr."

Many other distinguished guests visited Petersburg, one of the most famous being Edgar Allan Poe.

In 1836, he and Virginia Clemm, his child bride, spent their honeymoon here. They stayed at Haines' Restorative or Coffee House, called by Edward Wyatt (*Along Petersburg Streets*) "A Tavern for Poets."

BOLLING HOUSE — *Hospitality has abounded in Petersburg where doors of stately homes have opened to generations of famous guests. In this handsome residence on Sycamore Street, General Lee attended the wedding reception of his son, General W. H. F. Lee, and Miss Mary Tabb Bolling.*

Hiram Haines was a poet in his own right, and his Coffee House a gathering place for literary personalities.

Poe and his little Virginia were given a Petersburg welcome. For two weeks of his storm-tossed life Poe found a haven. The happy couple were wined and dined. All went merry as a marriage bell, and perhaps the poet's heart was singing:

> Hear the mellow wedding bells,
>   Golden Bells!
> What a world of happiness their harmony foretells!
>   Through the balmy air of night
>   How they ring out their delight!
>   All in tune,
>   What a liquid ditty floats
> To the turtle-dove that listens, while she gloats
>   On the moon!

Other literary visitors came to Petersburg. Thackeray was here in 1853 and lectured on "The Four Georges."

The drama was also represented. The mother and father of Edgar Allan Poe were here for a theatrical engagement. And Junius Brutus Booth played Richard III on his second appearance in America — his first was in Richmond. On a hot, July day he missed the "coach" and walked to Petersburg! He was not too tired to tread the boards when he got here, however, and gave a magnificent performance.

Another distinguished guest was Sidney Lanier. This much-loved Southern Poet, not only sang for us, but fought for us. He was with General Lee at Violet Bank in Colonial Heights. Here Sunday services were held under the gigantic cucumber tree in the yard, the hymns punctuated by the boom of cannon.

On a warm summer day during service Mr. Lanier noticed that the General had dropped to sleep. And, said the poet, General Lee was as majestic in repose as in action.

At Moss's Tavern, Alexander A. Stephens and President Jefferson Davis were guests. The President was here on the way to take charge of the Confederate Government in Richmond.

In 1867, the most welcome visitor we've ever had, was and is, Robert E. Lee! The occasion was the marriage of his son, General W. H. F. Lee to

Miss Mary Tabb Bolling. This was the General's first public appearance after the surrender.

General Lee arrived at the station, at the foot of Sycamore Street. There was an impressive carriage waiting to take him to the Mahone residence (now the Public Library) where he was to spend the night.

But the horses stamping with impatience did not draw the carriage up the street. General Lee's "boys," who had followed him to Appomattox, unhitched the horses and claimed the dear privilege of pulling the carriage themselves.

We have welcomed guests throughout the years with triumphal arches, with fanfare and flowers.

The flowers have faded, but this affectionate gesture to Marse Robert still lives, for it is rooted and grounded in our hearts. Petersburg remembers.

Coming down to recent history — well, fifty years ago — we had a very fine party for President William Howard Taft.

It was May when wistaria was trailing its lavender veils over the trees, and ladies were trailing their loveliest gowns over the lawn of Centre Hill.

The party, which belongs to the history of Centre Hill Mansion, produced, among other momentoes, a handsome program. It is dated May 19, 1909 — Visit of William Howard Taft, President of the United States, and Mrs. Taft.

The occasion was the unveiling of a monument erected by the State of Pennsylvania to the Third Division, of the Ninth Army Corps of the Army of the Potomac, at Fort Mahone.

Tucked in among pictures of Petersburg in the program is a list of visitors to Petersburg for over three hundred years. It goes from Powhatan to President Taft, and lists:

Opechancanough
Pocahontas
John Smith
Sir Thomas Dale
Governor Spotswood
Colonel William Byrd, of Westover

Lord Cornwallis
  General O'Hara
   General Phillips
    Colonel Simcoe
     Benedict Arnold
      General Lafayette
       Baron Steuben

George Washington
  Patrick Henry
   John Burk
    Thomas Jefferson

James Madison
  James Monroe
   John Randolph, of Roanoke
    John Tyler
     Marquis de Chastellux
      Winfield Scott

William Henry Harrison
  Franklin Pierce
   Abraham Lincoln
    Jefferson Davis
     U. S. Grant
      A. P. Hill

P. G. T. Beauregard
  James Longstreet
   A. E. Burnside
    John B. Gordon
     William Makepeace Thackeray
      Marquis of Lorne

J. J. Jusserand, Ambassador of France
  Charles D. Sigsbee
   William Howard Taft

A welcome, like wine, mellows with age. For several centuries Petersburg has happily received her guests. Through Colonial days, Revolutionary days, the War between the States, the First World War and the Second World War.

In April, 1917, Camp Lee sprang up, as if by magic, at Hopewell just three miles from Petersburg.

Here, under General Adelbert Cronkhite, the famous 80th Division trained. There was a troop capacity of over 60,000 men. They claimed Petersburg for their "home away from home," and Petersburg loved them. The "doughboys" invited the girls to dances at Camp Lee, the girls invited the soldiers to dinner at home. These were exciting days — with Dan Cupid not marking time, but making it.

In 1939, World War II began in Europe and storm clouds drifted over the Atlantic. In 1940, another Camp Lee sprang into being. At the peak of activity, 35,000 men were undergoing training.

And finally, in 1950, Camp Lee became a permanent installation of the Department of the Army. As Fort Lee it is now the Quartermaster Training Command.

Many permanent buildings have been added through the years; a library, a theatre, and enlarged quarters for men and officers.

Somewhere near the center of activity is The Court of the Nation. A green rectangle of grass is surrounded by fifty flags for fifty states, and one more for the District of Columbia. On a sunny day the brave colors stand out to the wind — new colors that have woven themselves into Old Glory.

The boys from Fort Lee still walk our streets. The uniforms have changed but the soldiers haven't. They come from every state, and Virginia, the "Mother of States," welcomes them home.

GENTLEMEN, YOU MAY SMOKE

HESE WORDS, or a reasonable facsimile, were first spoken by an American to Columbus more than four hundred years ago. When Columbus landed at San Salvador, he was greeted by some friendly Indians, who with true southern hospitality, invited him to smoke. They offered a bit of tobacco rolled in a dried leaf — the aboriginal cigarette.

Some years later, when Edward VII became King of England, he joined his male guests in the coffee room after the first formal banquet. Queen Victoria had frowned on smoking, so it was with surprise and pleasure that the guests listened to King Edward, "Gentlemen, you may smoke."

This welcome invitation has been accepted around the world.

Virginia has been interested in the cultivation of the "bewitching vegetable," as William Byrd called it, since John Rolfe's experiments at Jamestown in 1612. He combined some South American seed with the native tobacco. "Never," says one writer, "was marriage of soil and seed more fruitful. In these great leaves was wealth beyond the gold of the Aztecs or the mines of Peru."

In the early days of the Colony tobacco did everything. It was coin of the realm. It bought a wife for 120 pounds. This was a strictly imported article from England, a young woman of "virtuous education" (says the commercial) and "the price of a wife shall have precedence over all debts . . . because this merchandise of all other shall be most desirable."

Tobacco supported the family through life and in death. When the good man of the house came to the end of the furrow, the parson (and 400 pounds of tobacco) would bury him in the good Virginia soil from which the United States has sprung.

Over in England Sir Walter Raleigh had set the fashion for young men to "drink smoke," as they did in Virginia.

One day (you remember) Sir Walter's servant found the smoke pouring out of his master, and doused him with a can of ale.

But one can of ale couldn't quench the flame, and soon smoke rings wreathed the world.

Many V.I.P.'s tried to stop it. Among them King James I of England. He issued a "Counterblaste to Tobacco," and regaled his subjects with the evils of the stuff — "It makes us wallow in all sorts of idle thoughts."

Perhaps some "idle thoughts" were needed to combat the rugged days of the seventeenth century, or the tense ones of the twentieth.

In any case, where there was so much smoke there must be some fire — wild fire. It leaped ahead in many guises. It became a wonder drug. It was called the Sovereign Remedy, and cured everything from poverty to the plague.

In 1650, a page employed by Jean Nicot, French Ambassador to Portugal, brought word of the amazing curative properties of tobacco. Nicot sent some seeds to the Queen Mother of France, Catherine d'Medici. A poultice, they said, would cure headaches — and France had plenty of those. And so they called the stuff Nicotine.

Well, whatever they called it, it came high. It was worth its weight, if not in gold, in good silver shillings. And its importance in the fiscal affairs of England grew in magnitude.

In 1691, Commissary James Blair went to England to obtain a charter for the proposed college at Williamsburg. The Queen was willing, the King was willing, and a grant of two thousand pounds sterling was authorized.

But Sir Edward Seymour, who was to draw the charter, objected. There was a war on and he needed tobacco taxes to win it.

In vain did James Blair plead that the new college would prepare men for the ministry — Virginia had souls that needed saving . . .

"Damn your souls," thundered Sir Edward, "make tobacco!"

James Blair did. He had his head in the clouds, but his feet were in a tobacco field. He got 20,000 acres of land, where John Rolfe's alchemy turned the mighty leaf to gold, and higher education got its start in Virginia.

The first experiments of the colonists were open to improvement. The tobacco was described as "poore and weake, and of a byting taste." John Rolfe said it needed a little more "triall and expense."

The "triall" worked out, and, in 1617, 20,000 pounds of tobacco were exported from Virginia.

DONNAN HOUSE — *Built between 1770 and 1790 by a Frenchman named Rombeau, this fine residence was purchased in 1847 by the present owner's ancestor who was a tobacco and cotton broker. This broker came to Petersburg from Wink Wigtonshire, Scotland.*

Today we do a little better. It is said that Virginia produces enough of the "golden weed" each year to make one long cigarette that would stretch fifty times around the world. (Melvin Herndon, *Tobacco in Colonial Virginia*.)

But this didn't happen between puffs. The history of tobacco is a history of trial and error, of struggle, defeat, and victory.

When John Rolfe began his experiments in tobacco, he wrote a new page in history. The mighty leaf was to shape our lives then and now. It is a palimpsest on which the history of Virginia is written.

In the Capitol at Washington, there is a small court surrounded by picturesque columns, crowned with graceful, curving capitals, a tobacco leaf. These columns are as interesting and ornamental, if not as elaborate, as the Corinthian.

Surely no more fitting design for Virginia could have been conceived. This sturdy leaf was to uphold the economy of Virginia then and now.

From 1611 the history of tobacco is the history of Virginia.

It turned men into manufacturers, and trading stations into cities. It made the plantations, and the planters — the Fitzhughs, Byrds, Carters, Randolphs, Harrisons, Nelsons, Lees, and others — made history.

The tiny seed that grew into the mighty leaf made a trading station into Petersburg. About eighteen years before it was formally established as a town it became a center for marketing tobacco.

Warehouses were established. In 1769, Roger Atkinson, of Mansfield, could say that there was more tobacco in Petersburg warehouses than "in all York River besides from head to foot."

And an English traveller wrote, "The streets of Petersburg were crowded with hogsheads of tobacco, and on the road we continually met with single hogsheads, drawn by horses, coming eighty or a hundred miles from the interior."

They had to get the tobacco to market, hence the development of roads. They chose the highest ground to avoid creeks and lowgrounds. This accounts for the meandering roads of the present day — the Boydton Plank Road, the Jerusalem Plank Road, a triumph of means over mud.

Along these roads came the "tobacco rollers," rolling and singing. They put an iron bar through the center of the barrels and with a song on their lips were on their way.

On the river the boatmen were bringing their tobacco, in flat-bottomed bateaux. They rowed as they sang:

> Oh, I'm gwine down to town!
> An' I'm gwine down to town!
> I'm gwine down to Richmond town
>   (or Petersburg town, or Lynchburg town)
> To cyar my 'bacca down.

The warehouses were referred to as "rolling houses." Their receipts were used for money, as paper currency is today.

In 1856, a northern visitor said: "I have visited some of the large manufactories, where they have from one to two hundred slaves at work — twisting and pressing the weed. Sometime one will give out with a hymn, when all strike up a lively tune, keeping time with their work; and I can assure you that the music would put to blush many of our northern singing circles."

Before the Revolution it was the custom of planters to sell direct to European purchasers. This gave way later to "factors," foreign agents stationed in the colonies. Some of these played an important part in Petersburg's early days.

The first manufacturers, largely Scotch, operated the warehouses and factories. Among the early names were: Ashton Johnson, Robert Leslie, and his nephews, Robert L. Watson from Scotland, and John McGill from Canada; James Dunlop — a native of Scotland who established a large business here, to be followed by relatives who were to become leading figures in the industry; David Brydon, whose nephew, Brydon Tennant, was in business with the Dunlops.

There were three Cameron brothers, William, Alexander, and George, who came to Petersburg in the first half of the nineteenth century.

To list all who made tobacco history in Petersburg is impossible in so short a space but we mention a few: Samuel Woodson Venable, Thomas Branch, Reuben Ragland, James McCuloch, Peter McEnery, James Chieves, Edmund Harrison Osborne, and James Orr.

By 1836, Petersburg had six tobacco factories, and soon the manufacture of tobacco became the city's principal industry. Dr. John Herbert Claiborne could write that in 1850, "Tobacco was king."

It has been said that tobacco is as American as Indians or apple pie. But the uses of it have varied with men and nations.

England and America liked the pipe. Then came snuffing, "chawing," the "segar," and finally, *quote* "a more feminine article delicately nominated cigarette."

Everybody wanted to get into the act: poets, dramatists, artists.

James M. Barrie says: "The introduction of tobacco awoke England from a long sleep. The glory of existence became a thing to speak of. Men put a pipe in their mouths and became philosophers."

One of these was Sir Walter Raleigh. It was said of him: "He tooke a pipe of Tobacco a little before he went to the scaffold, which some formall persons were scandalized at, but I thinke, 'twas well and properly done, to settle his spirits."

In lighter vein, another devotee waxed lyric over the "smoke blossom," as the Chinese called it — "the herb of amiability."

> The daintiest dish of a delicious feast,
> By taking which man differs from the beast . . .
> All goods, all pleasures it in one doth link,
> 'Tis physic, music, meat and drink.

Certainly, it was music. From seed time to harvest, through manufacture, many a song has gone into it. The English composer, Delius, has left us *Appalachia,* founded on a tune he got from the tobacco stemmery in Danville, Virginia.

In the old days, in the tobacco factories, someone would "line out" a hymn, or a spiritual, or folk song, and out would come the music, out would come the work.

The eighteenth century sneezed itself through England. Snuffing was the order of the day. The man about town was not properly turned out without his snuff box. These were elaborate gold and silver affairs, sparkling with many jewels.

They were often carried in the head of a cane, when with lace ruffles falling from a velvet sleeve, a gay blade offered it to his lady love.

"Chawing" did not do so well in England, but it was prevalent in the United States. Some of the brands manufactured in Petersburg were described in a monograph by Robert Barton called (and we quote) *Plug Tobacco and High Art.*

"Real Art," says Mr. B., had its hey-day fifty or seventy years ago. Then there were wooden Indians, masterpieces of wood carving.

And, of course, there were cigarette pictures (the pin-up girls of yesterday), actresses billowing in wreaths of smoke — football players, baseball players, and an occasional Indian chief.

In Petersburg, there were good names like "Pluck" — our hero holds a sword in one hand, a pistol in the other, as another hated redskin bit the dust.

Romance is given with "First Kiss," a gent with a straw hat on his head, a lady in his arms, and, no doubt, a fine bit of plug in his pocket. The "Kohinoor," a diamond-shaped picture of the man in the gray flannel suit, plus top hat and puff tie — has this caption:

> Rich and rare were the Oaths he swore,
> And the Kohinoor in his breast he wore.

"Chawing" was followed, of course, by "segars." These were a sort of tobacco who's who — the man of distinction was hardly so without his fat, fragrant, brown cigar.

True, some of the lesser breed defined a cigar as having "a fire on one end, a fool on the other."

But no less a person than Rudyard Kipling summed up boy-meets-girl theme with this line:

> And a woman is only a woman
> But a good cigar is a smoke.

This gentlemen's view of things was held in Petersburg in our childhood. Grandpas and uncles and gentlemen generally smoked cigars.

And that meant to the small fry treasure unspeakable — cigar boxes! We used them for everything. The boys housed their precious collections of bird eggs; the girls kept their doll clothes in the little cedar chests.

In Richmond, a collection of Indian arrow heads was kept in cigar boxes. These were the beginning of the Valentine Museum.

At long last, after a hundred years war over it, ladies began to smoke. This was, of course, that article "delicately denominated cigarette."

In Petersburg, we make these "feminine articles" in a big way. We use for these trifles sixty million pounds of tobacco a year.

A pack-by-pack account would take you to a big tobacco factory. Again there's a song, keeping time, time, time, in a sort of Runic rhyme, the song of machinery. The all-but-human machines put in the tobacco, cut off the cigarette, package it from spools of white and silver, and tie them with a red ribbon of cellophane.

The packs jump into boxes, in an unbroken cadence — packs, packs, packs, packs . . . One hundred and twenty a minute.

As an accompaniment to the song of the machines there is the sweet smell of tobacco, toasted with rum and syrups, and goodness knows what else. As with any good chef, the recipe is not given away.

It reminded us of an old Negro cook. When we admired a particularly good dish, and asked for the recipe (we call it *receipt*), she said: "I don't use no deceit — I jes' goes accordin' to conscience."

We assume the Petersburg manufacturer does the same thing, since the end result, we are told, tastes "good."

The sweet smell of toasting tobacco is not confined to the factory. The air of the city is permeated with it. And a very nostalgic smell it is — a warm, brown, molassesy smell.

It is Petersburg's theme smell. Perhaps we'd best settle for an early brand of Virginia's golden weed, and call it "Sweet Scented."

That's the atmosphere of today and yesterday. It is an aromatic echo of an old, old invitation: "Gentlemen, you may smoke."

PAINT AND PRIDE

"**P**ETERSBURG," says a friendly enemy, "is the place where they are too poor to paint and too proud to whitewash." Well . . . Maybe we could do with a spot of paint here and there, but we couldn't do without our pride. Petersburg, among other cities in the United States, has been designated an ALL-AMERICAN CITY.

We feel (with all due modesty, of course!) that we deserve this accolade.

If it means putting the best foot forward, keeping up with the best in city planning, we think we qualify. And if it means being willing to fight for our convictions, we know we do.

Petersburg has never failed to accept a challenge. From the days of Fort Henry in 1645, when we were trading beads and blows with the Indians — all the way from Canada (1812) to Korea — we've been in there punching. For three hundred years we've never missed a fight.

We are proud of this record. Pride is more important than paint; and whitewash is nothing but defeat.

One of Petersburg's ladies of an old family (about two hundred years old) puts it this way: "My dear," she says, "never mend a run in your stocking. If a tear is noticed while you are out, that is an accident that might happen to anybody, but if you mend it, that is *premeditated poverty!*"

And so is whitewash. The old silver-gray clapboards draw their ivy mantles about them, and with patience and dignity await their new coat of paint. But whitewash — a defeatist attitude at best, and its worst — premeditated poverty!

Poverty, like most things, is comparative.

After the "wah" (War between the States, that is) it was a disgrace to have any money. If you had had any, it had been, of course, turned into Confederate bonds. As long as nobody had much money, the difference between people was negligible, and life went on in the old tradition. We had "Starvation Balls," but we still danced.

For Petersburg loves parties, and she loves "company." We are convinced that "The man who came to dinner" came from Petersburg!

Visitors came and visitors stayed — and stayed. One lady ("Aunt Jerushy," we called her) came to supper and stayed two years.

In the "visiting nineties" this was not too unusual.

A young friend of ours was visiting relatives in the country. Her glamour as a "visiting girl" began to dim, and her hostess thought an explanation was in order. "You see," she said, "my dear niece is *money-bound.*"

Visiting, with some of the "maiden ladies" at the turn of the century, was a career. They went to the country in the summer when it was hot, and to the city in the winter when it was not.

And some of the dear old girls were not without a bit of guile. Cousin Mollie (everybody was "cousin" something) had a very handsome diamond ring. When she was staying with us she said she was going to leave it to the daughter of the house.

Everywhere she went she let drop the same delightful hint. For years she visited on that diamond ring. (None of us got it.)

Entertaining went on in the dignified style of the day. "The Gentlemen's Club" was organized by a small group for two purposes only: good food and good talk.

It was strictly a stag affair, but we peeped through the pantry door. There was terrapin stew, made by the steward at the Petersburg Club, across the street, by a famous recipe. There were partridges, stuffed like miniature turkeys, or sora (which we didn't call reed birds) on toast, and good to the last bone. There was Sally Lunn, a fluted, golden brown mound. Mint juleps started the supper, brandy finished it, and wine flowed between. After coffee, long, thin Havana cigars.

When these were going, the gentlemen sat back, fragrant, blue smoke wreathing their silver heads. Someone would clear his throat and say, "I recollect in the spring of '63 . . ."

Again the bugles were calling.

It didn't matter if outside the paint was wearing a little thin; inside, the hospitality wasn't.

In words of our mountain neighbors, the old house "sits mighty easy."

"THE LADIES—GOD BLESS 'EM"

HIS TOAST, in the old days, was the first in any large social gathering. But times have changed, perhaps in nothing more than the almost obsolete term: Ladies. But we used to have them. Dignity, wit, wisdom, charm and gaiety. You could always tell a lady by her gaiety, her handkerchief and her white kid gloves.

Dignity, perhaps, came first. A black silk dress, white ruching at the neck, held in place with a brooch, or maybe grandpa's hair framed in a gold breastpin. Milady's hair was parted in the middle, drawn back in undeviating "crimps" on each side, topped by a bonnet trimmed with feathers or maybe jet, bobbing about like black hail.

With polished shoes (ladies always put the best foot forward) and white gloves, she was ready to go visiting.

This was something of an art, and practiced to perfection in Petersburg. It was sympathy, sociability, and news gathering all in one. News flashed via station Grapevine almost as quickly as it does by radio today.

"Did you hear, my dear, that Sally Smith — " a sibilant whisper. (That must have been a juicy morsel, filtered sotto voce through a black silk fan.)

Some visitors called morning, noon, and night, and did little else. One of them was telling the Negro cook that she (the mistress) would help out when the cook went on her vacation — then Cook: "And what could *you* do? What is you ever done but *set*, and rock and put on your white gloves and go visiting?"

Visiting was an important ritual. Besides the white gloves there was a silver cardcase, with cards which were bent at the corner or in the middle, according to the best pre-Emily Post tradition. Every little bend had a meaning all its own.

On a pleasant day milady went calling in a victoria. Everything was shining — the horse, the harness and the high hat of the Negro on the box.

The victoria, or landau, drew up to the carriage stone and the lady lifted her trailing skirts and stepped in. When it was sunny she raised her parasol, a dainty trifle of silk, that tilted to keep the sun out of her eyes.

If the weather was chilly a carriage stone, pre-heated on the kitchen range, was carefully placed beneath her slippered feet. The stone had an iron bar running through it for handling. Ladies of the nineteenth century went calling in comfort.

So did ladies of the twentieth century. In the early days of motor cars the horseless carriage was also heatless. So on a cold day when we went to Richmond we heated grandma's stone, carefully wrapped it in a blanket, and kept warm all the way.

On the return trip, after dinner at a hotel, we tipped the bell boy — he "het up" the stone again — and we kept warm all the way to Petersburg.

There was more time for visiting at the turn of the century. A lady's activities were inside, not outside the home. Her garden club was a private affair in the back yard, with Mistress Columbine, Marechal Niel and General Jacqueminot.

The P.T.A. was a parent-teacher (all one word) association that met in the dining room five nights a week. Here lessons were studied with aid and comfort from the head of the table.

Domestic visiting, however, paled into insignificance when the foreign variety, meaning the country cousins, arrived. This was something of an art, or should we say an avocation.

Unattached ladies, the sisters, and the cousins, and the aunts, moved in an undeviating schedule, as regular as the flight of wild geese. Certain homes were good for winter, others for spring, and, of course, you wound up in the country in August, with the corn and tomatoes and butterbeans, and Brunswick Stew.

Ladies never went to market. It was considered unrefined to "haggle with hucksters." It was also unrefined to look a beefsteak in the face.

The head of the family took a market basket and sallied forth. Later the basket came back loaded (if the gentleman was ditto, he had stopped for a quick one with a friend) and almost bursting its slats. Slightly inebriated delicacies jostled the sober potatoes, and menus were fitted to the mood of the master of the market basket.

When we did go shopping it was an exciting experience for a little girl. We sauntered forth, holding grandma's hand — sauntered is the word — ladies never hurried.

Down Sycamore Street we went, through narrow defiles, flanked on each side by great burlap bales of cotton. They looked like fat old ladies with bits of cotton sticking out, held in place by "stays" of steel. There were huge bags of peanuts, the earthy peanutty smell permeating the air, as the sacks were wheeled off on trucks, a Negro smiling and pushing.

We passed the swinging doors of a "Fancy Grocery," where even more fancy goods were sold over the bar at the back. The swinging door would burst open ("Don't look in there, Kate") and out would come a cheerful gentleman and a smell of beer, happily blended.

Then the bakers . . . Such delectable cakes in the window — snowballs, pound cake inside, white icing outside, and bridal cakes, looking to us like the Empire State Building does now. And that warm sweet smell of hot bread which nostalgically assaults the nostrils of the world. A common denominator of peoples — who can forget Tolstoi's description — perhaps with united noses we could do better with united nations.

We went shopping — grandma chatting graciously with acquaintances, and I watching fascinated, as a little box overhead ran around the store and came back with the right change — this pre-I.B.M. was as mysterious to me as the mastermind machine of today.

We were waited on by a gentleman, of course. The right to work was not exercised by the bustled sex. News flash, later: "Did you hear that they have a *lady* clerk at Scoggin's?"

We looked at shoes, but try them on? Heaven forbid! Grandma picked some out, to be tried on in the privacy of the lower chamber, at home, else a horrid secret might have been revealed: Ladies have legs!

They didn't in Petersburg. Cheesecake was strictly a product of the kitchen and not of the front page. A lady's slippers were hitched to her dresses, of course. As the poet has it:

> Her feet beneath her petticoat,
> Like little mice stole in and out.

So, pretty soon a boy would appear with traps for the little mice — a huge pile of white boxes, like the leaning tower of Pisa, black face peeking out.

SILVER SETT — *This handsome service was created about 1840 in New York by H. Salisbury and Co. for a Petersburg lady. The floral decoration was copied from an imported china tea set. The silversmiths reported that it "... has the credit here of being the handsomest set of silver ever made in New York."*

If the shoe proved to be Cinderella's own, it was bought at once. But, maybe if it didn't quite — oh well, with a little squeezing — ladies never wore more than size one-and-a-half — and with the buttons moved, perhaps — Vanity, and high cloth-tops covered many a fallen arch.

Getting a dress was not any quick trick in the Ready Wear department. Much time and thought were spent in getting the right materials.

Samples were brought home and subjected to rigorous tests. If the stuff was cotton, the bright colors were suspect. They were subjected to hard washing to see if they'd *run*. Only the most sedentary pieces were countenanced in that era.

If the dress was for winter, serge was the stand-by, or perhaps lady's cloth. And for *best* there was mozambique, surah and satin, and peau de soie. Tucks, puffs, buttons and bows for decor, or most elegant of all, a bit of passamentarie.

All the specifications having been met, lining, whalebone, hooks and eyes, plus the dress-length of material, we went to the mantua maker, dressmaker to you.

This was Miss Indie (short for India) who was our Dior in petticoats. She was soft, round and comfortable, with her apron over her black alpaca dress, a tomato pincushion pinned to her side. She and the pincushion were much the same shape.

The amenities, the health of the ladies disposed of, trying on began. Meanwhile, a treasure hunt for paper dolls went on in the corner with the side-table set, *Demarest's,* the *Delineator,* perhaps an old *Godey's Lady's Book,* were searched for pictures. Some were in color, simpering ladies with bows, bustles and feather boas, flanked by tall-hatted gentlemen, as boy meets girl.

After lots of talk, lots of pins, some fitting, the visit came to an end. The precious "scraps" were picked up, destined for dresses for our dolls, shortly to be initiated into the Dinsmore family. In later years when I came across some Dinsmores in the sacred precincts of a New England churchyard, I could hardly refrain from dropping a tear. Alas, I knew them well.

When the dress was finished, complete with boned bodice, yards and yards of skirt, even more yards of dust ruffling, it was brought home like a baby, carefully wrapped in snowy towels.

Of course, all this, the dainty shoes, the pretty dress, naturally led to the old feminine custom of setting one's cap for a beau. The successful culmination of this (times don't really change much in Cupid's calendar) was a proposal. The "this-is-so-sudden" school of thought prevailed, though how any nit-wit could have mistaken the "attentions" is a mystery. The proposer was told to come back the next night for his answer.

On such a night, a suitor called to see my great-aunt. He was shown into the parlor, stiff with mahogany and horsehair, and the atmosphere as cold as the white marble mantelpiece.

And, in no time at all, he was shown out. Nobody needed to be told what happened. But why in the world wasn't the lad given the old heave-ho on the first night?

Ah, well. These matters were conducted with dignity, and decorum. Perhaps they had something. They didn't jump into marriage, and also, they didn't jump out. Husbands seemed to wear better, and there was more mileage in matrimony.

Husbands were addressed by their wives, as "mister" so and so. We thought that odd, and when we inquired we were told by our uncle that it would not be respectful for his wife to call him "Jim." All a build-up for dignity, and perhaps dignity, like virtue, is its own reward.

MANNERS, strictly uppercase, were paramount. One stickler said she really thought they were more important than morals! Perhaps that was overstating it, but maybe the line is closer than we think, and manners and dignity a sort of antibiotic for slipshod behavior. The fear of loss of dignity, has, perhaps, saved many a high hat from low moments.

Don't think that ladies were always soft. There was a hard core of determination that held the lines in social behavior. Things must be done "just so." The velvet glove could conceal a pointed barb, and when occasion demanded, an impertinent bubble was instantly pricked. "No lady," said a grande dame, "is ever unintentionally rude."

Nearly everybody was called "Miss." This was a term of affection and had nothing to do with the number of a lady's husbands.

"Miss Sally," "Miss Phronie," "Miss Tish" (for Letitia) and in one case a grandmother, called "Baby" at home, was addressed as "Miss Baby" by everybody else.

92

STRACHAN-HARRISON HOUSE — *Situated thirteen stone steps above Cross Street behind Grace Church, this house was once used for a children's school and later as a parish house. Built by Dr. Alexander G. Strachan, a Scotchman, in 1735, the house was described as a setting by Miss Ellen Glasgow in her novel,* VIRGINIA.

There were a lot of big and littles — "Big Mamma," the matriarch of one family, "Little Mamma," in a four-generation menage, and practically everybody was cousin something. There was a sense of belonging in all this that was like a warm, encircling arm around the old city.

All the "aunts" were not in the parlor. The colored members of the household, the cooks, the housemaids, the washwomen, and the nurses were called "aunt" — "Aunt Cindy," "Aunt Liza," "Aunt Maria."

This was a title of affection and respect. For the trundle-bed trash in the nursery, it was authority personified. We had to mind, or else.

My own nurse was "Aunt Fanny." Tall, with a proud carriage, and a face like a Roman coin, she was a tyrant, though a benevolent one. She raised me, or tried to. "Little ladies" do this — "little ladies" don't do that — and on, and on, and on.

One day rebellion raised its ugly head, even a lady worm will turn. I "spit" at "Aunt Fanny."

And the spanking my mother gave me for that I'll remember to my dying day. Rudeness and disobedience were bad enough with the white "aunts." But with the colored ones there was only one punishment to fit the crime — the uncompromising side of a hair brush.

The languishing female of the Victorian novels, who had the vapors on the least provocation, was not a lady in our sense of the word.

A lady was a soldier of society. She kept her feelings down, her head up, and she held on. Come hell or high water, poverty, sickness, tragedy and bereavement, she met the world. A lady might be down, but she was never out. She brought up her family by guts and grace.

After the war — the one between the States, of course — poverty was the order of the day. But not a topic of conversation. Money was a dirty word — ladies didn't mention it — it wasn't genteel to talk about the horrid stuff.

And though poverty came in by the door, culture did not fly out of the window. One of my early memories is of the magnificent mother of a no-money family. When she had to take her turn in the kitchen on cook's day off, she brought the parlor with her, or rather, the library. She cooked, she stirred, she read. If a long-handled spoon was in her right hand, a classic was in her left. For years I associated Dickens with vegetable soup.

And though there was not much variety on the supper table, there were the crocheted mats, starched and stretched to lace-like cobwebs, with the old walnut table showing through, the blue Canton china, and always room for one more.

There was plenty of batterbread, and damson preserves in a red glass dish. At the head of the table was the hostess with the silver hair and the golden heart, and rippling down the board was laughter, lovely laughter. Nobody had time to think there was nothing much (if anything at all) in the covered dish at the foot of the table — there was so much happiness in between.

This practice of make-do was a fine art with Virginia's first families, down to their last dollar.

The ladies turned the curtains, and made over their dresses, but one thing remained intact: tradition.

There was plenty of this, and protocol was the order of the day.

We came out, we went in, we got married, all according to what "was done." Particularly was this true of funerals. Funeral directors are supposed to be men, but behind every frock-coated official was a lady in black bombazine and veils.

Mourning was not only a matter of dress but of decorum. The house was kept in stygian darkness — the piano could not be opened — music had no charms for the crepe-trimmed savage breast.

A lady who had had a death in the family went out shrouded in black from head to toe, her heavy veil sweeping to the bottom of her skirt. On the hottest July day she trailed down Sycamore Street — mourning was a matter of temperament, not temperature, and ladies did not perspire.

If milady wore widow's weeds, she had a small pointed bonnet ruched with white, and vastly becoming.

So becoming that one pretty widow got two proposals the same day. Mistress Cicely Jordan, a lovely lady from a neighboring county and an earlier day, was long on charm but short on timing.

"They say" that the parson and the undertaker both proposed and someway . . .

Well — the upshot of this widow's wiles caused the Governor and Council to issue a stern edict forbidding a woman's engaging herself to two men at once. There is no record in Virginia indicating that this was ever revoked.

After a year or two ladies lightened their mourning. This was called second mourning; a coming out in gentle colors, gray, lavender and so on. The ignorant male didn't always understand this. When one of them was told that "Miss Sarah" had gone in second mourning, in a distressed voice came the question, "Who is dead now?"

When a lady finally emerged from her chrysalis — if a widow and she was "taking notice" — she got a hat with flowers on it. One of these went to a funeral — not on the lady's head, since it was a bit gay for such a sad occasion. The lady wore her old black hat, and carefully placed the rose-covered number beside her in the pew. (She was stepping out after the funeral.)

It was the custom for the friends of the family to carry the floral offerings to the cemetery; no florist's van in the offing in those days.

So when the procession moved down the aisle to the door of the church, one of the members picked up the floral arrangement by milady's side in the corner of the pew.

She could only follow sadly behind the cortege, and take a last lingering look at her pretty hat, as it descended slowly into the good earth.

The lady didn't mourn over this; she made a funny story out of it. To see the humorous side was one of the bulwarks of society. "There's always something funny about everything," the ladies would say.

They mourned, but they did not despair. Their sense of proportion, and their sense of the ridiculous, that blessing of the South, kept them on an even keel. They were — that lovely word just made for ladies — serene.

We hear much today of facing facts. But the ladies — God bless 'em — redeemed them.

. . . AND GENTLEMEN

O VIRGINIA GENTLEMAN," said one of them in the gay nineties, "ever expects to be warm all around at the same time. He warms his front and then he turns and warms his back." This rotisserie method was in effect in my childhood. Is it any wonder the hearth stands for the center of activity?

Gentlemen were first of all — hosts. The guest was made happy no matter what happened in the house, or to the householder.

A friend of ours had a handsome pair of cut glass decanters. While gathered around the sideboard, a guest through some horrible mischance, knocked one off and broke it.

And before you could say "jigger," the host broke the other. Glass sparkled like jewels over the floor, but the immediate jewel of his soul, the obligation to save the feelings of the guest, was saved.

This may seem to us an empty gesture. But in those genial times a graceful gesture was the order of the day. It was more a matter of heart than of hands.

I still remember the sweeping bow of the gentlemen as their hats came off. It took no imagination to see a waving plume sweeping the pavement. Chivalry walked our streets.

Our knights had no suits of shining armor, but they did have Prince Albert coats. These were worn with a puff tie, a scarf pin, striped "britches," and a high hat. This "beaver" was brushed to a beautiful lustre, with a tiny plush cushion — much in demand for pillows for our dolls.

Hospitality was as much a part of a Virginia gentleman as mint juleps, cigars, and the Prince Albert coat.

Hospitality is where the heart is. Respect, friendship, congenial tastes swung back the wide doors of the houses, but they didn't open to every casual knock.

A man's home was his castle, with a moat to be bridged. Money wouldn't do it. Even before the war, money, per se, had its limitations.

Dr. Herbert Claiborne in *Seventy-five Years in Old Virginia* says: "Money with its meretricious adornments and its vulgar displays was not the sesame to open any gentleman's door."

One of the principal meeting places was the Petersburg Club. It was a dignified, mellow brick, Georgian house just across the street from my great-grandfather's home.

Here politics, news, gossip, toddies and terrapin stew were dispensed, and sometimes went on and on.

When politics were getting hot — and our dinner getting cold — a servant went out on our porch and rang a big brass dinner bell.

This was a summons with authority, and eventually the men folk of the house struggled down the high stone steps of the Club, and up ours, with the eloquence of several mint juleps to bolster their excuses.

When a gentleman sauntered out — high hat, frock coat, a goldheaded cane, he was impressive indeed. When the hat came off, it disclosed a fine head of hair. This did not stop with the top of the head, but went on into handsome beards. These were kept carefully trimmed, the process winding up with a dash of bay rum.

Which reminds me of a story. One day a gentleman called to see my uncle and Kenna, the butler cum-valet, let him in. While waiting for my uncle to appear Kenna did the honors. "A se-gar, suh?" he got the box out of the drawer in the library table.

"No, thank you," the visitor declined. "I don't smoke."

Kenna started toward the dining room and the sideboard — "A toddy, suh?"

"No," a decided shake of the head, "I don't drink."

Kenna pondered sadly, then "Excuse me, suh, but what does you do to make you smell like a gentleman?"

All the gentlemen did not have white skins. We cannot think of gentlemen without remembering Eddie Jones, the Negro janitor of the Petersburg Public Library.

Besides taking care of the Library, he took care of us, the staff. He was our guide, counsellor and friend. Always cheerful, his smiling face beamed out from the white froth of spiraea as he trimmed the bushes around the old gray-brown mansion.

One of Eddie's duties was to raise the flag.

One morning, our Congressman, who lived across the street, was surprised to see Old Glory upside down. He stopped to remonstrate with Eddie. "No, no, Eddie, you've got the flag upside down. That's a signal of distress."

Eddie's quick wit flashed out — "Yes, suh, we's in distress — two of our ladies is sick!"

Eddie felt his responsibilities. One of these was to uphold the dignity of the Library.

On one of the first days of a very raw assistant (myself) Eddie was dusting around the Library. He used a feather duster. He didn't care much for these new "ventilations" as another colored friend has it, and the vacuum cleaner was not his favorite tool. But he loved the feather duster. He wielded it with authority, much as a conductor does his baton.

A patron came in and asked for Robert's *Rules of Order*. I must have looked blank, and was heading for help in the catalog, when Eddie dusted over my way — "The little brown book on the top shelf-" the duster pointing like the needle to the Polar Star.

A friend presented the Library with an engraving of the Venus de Milo, and Eddie was helping to hang the picture.

The Librarian picked out a suitable place, but Eddie had other ideas. He thought it would look better behind the door. Finally, the Librarian sensed his unease, and so she explained, "You know, Eddie, this is a picture of a very famous lady of the olden times . . ."

"Yes'm," Eddie smiled as he saw the light, "she was a show lady!"

But Eddie was not all gamin. First, last, and always he was a gentleman. No matter how busy he was grass cutting, or pruning shrubs, or polishing the brass sign, when we spoke to him, off came his hat before he answered us.

He was wary, he was weatherwise. "Eddie, is it going to rain?" we would sometimes ask.

"Well, ma'am, wait 'twell I see some smoke," and when he did he could tell us, and his prediction was nearly always right. And if he smelled tobacco, it was *bound* to rain.

CHISOLM HOUSE — *Captain William Gordon McCabe, a paroled prisoner of war, settled in Petersburg in 1865 and founded his famous University School. This house was used as a dormitory.*

Eddie attended to our financial matters, brought our checks, made our purchases at the drug store, watched over us — I started to say like a mother, and I'm not sure that is not the word. He had an affectionate perception that we associate with that unselfish devotion.

The Librarian was struggling against an illness, which grieved us all. One day Eddie and I watched her come slowly across the street, the effort she was making sharply etched on her face.

"Oh, Eddie," I began, "I just can't bear to see her so weak . . ." I stopped, choked with tears.

Eddie looked not at me, but out of the window, as he answered something deeper than my thought, "Yes'm, but the way I looks at it, she is too brave to pity."

Eddie is gone now. But his kindness, his courtesy, his unfailing "gentlemanship" as one of his friends called it, is alive in our thoughts as long as we have them.

We are reminded of a story of a gentleman who did a colored brother a good turn, and the "brother" bestowed this accolade: "Deed, Mr. Mason, you is one good man — yes suh, you sho' is — your face is white but your heart is black!"

And so we wonder about Eddie — if the color scheme is important — his heart is white. Though come to think of it, we are, perhaps, presumptious to assume these distinctions. Kind hearts are more than color, and we loved Eddie just the way he was.

It is not hard to see reflections of knighthood in the gentlemen of the old school. "Gentlemanship" is only chivalry in modern dress.

A lady's escort still walks on the outside of the street, protecting her from goodness knows what terrors. He keeps his sword arm free, and his heart open. The strong must protect the weak.

My uncle had the honor of presiding over the Hustings Court for more than thirty years, and when he died was the last remaining Confederate soldier on the bench. In his long tour of duty he came in contact with much tragedy in human form. But somehow, he never became callous, and it was said that he tempered justice with mercy.

One evening we were in the library — an old room with tall walnut book cases, where Sir Walter Scott's knights rescued many a damsel in distress.

The firelight glinted on the green and gold bindings of the Waverley novels. It warmed my uncle's pink cheeks to a warmer hue below his silver hair, and above his silver beard.

He told me of a poor woman who had been evicted. She had nothing but a few of her bits and pieces left; however, she felt if she could just get down home to North Carolina she might make a fresh start. But she had no money, and was alone in the world.

"That's awful," I burst out, "could you do anything to help her?"

My uncle stooped over the fire, and with a paper lamp-lighter from the Japanese vase on the mantel, lit his cigar. He tossed the paper into the glowing embers and said, "I gave her a ticket home, and shipped her furniture."

"That was awfully good of you . . ." I began.

"Why, no . . ." Thoughtfully he regarded the end of his cigar, then between puffs he said, "what is life for?"

Gentlemen had names to suit their dignity, many of them of classical origin, Leonidas, Theophilus, and Ulysses.

"Ulysses" belonged to a gentleman who stayed with us through many weary months in 1864-65: Ulysses S. Grant.

Though uninvited, he left with us an impression of consideration and generosity which "bespoke the gentleman."

A son of Petersburg had the pleasure of meeting Maj. Gen. U. S. Grant, III, the General's grandson.

"General Grant," said the Petersburger, I have always wanted to meet a member of the Grant family. As the son of a good Confederate soldier, and the nephew of one who surrendered at Appomattox, I want to thank you for General Grant's magnanimous treatment of General Lee at Appomattox.

This General Grant smiled and said, "The old fellow was a gentleman, wasn't he?"

Another story is told of General Grant after he became President. At a social gathering in Washington, when the ladies had retired, and cigars were going, someone told an off-color story.

President Grant frowned.

Somewhat abashed, the story teller started to apologize, "After all, Mr. President, there are no ladies present."

"But gentlemen are," said Grant.

The president of a large manufacturing plant was once asked what was the most important product they turned out. And he said, "Men." Perhaps Petersburg's best product (next to *ladies,* of course) was gentlemen.

This began a long time ago, and was fostered by McCabe's University School, founded in 1865.

William Gordon McCabe was a boy, just out of the army, as he said, "a paroled prisoner of war with but one suit of clothes." He decided to try to make a living by opening a school. He began with seventeen boys.

For thirty-five years he taught them, and their sons. "From the foundation of the school Captain McCabe undertook to make it an exponent of excellence in two widely different directions; he set a premium on two things — high scholarship and high honor." (*Memories and Memorials of William Gordon McCabe* — Armistead Churchill Gordon.)

All of the lessons didn't come out of books. Quoting Mr. Gordon again: "When the spirit moved him, he had a way of saying 'Listen to me!' Every head was raised. 'I'll tell you about General Lee. You can't learn anything out of these fool histories.' "

"He would then talk of Lee . . . Often he would become so engrossed with the subject that the tears would roll down his cheeks. When the Old Man was thus delivering himself, the Masters would stand silently at their closed doors, but called no class. Boys returning from class would tiptoe to their seats, or stand like statues about the walls. For perhaps a half an hour he would talk. When he concluded, he would ordinarily gather up his books and say, 'Mr. Baker, take charge,' and leave amid perfect silence. Though his subject was always Lee, no two speeches were the same.

"If his ideal of education was Latin, and his ideal of manhood Robert E. Lee, his ideal institution of learning was the University. There could be but one, the whole world over, so why inquire which one?"

(We don't inquire, even now.)

When the Old Man called the roll, boys answered to names deep in the heart of Petersburg. Mr. Gordon gives this partial list: "D'Arcy Paul Roper, E. Leavenworth McGill, Hugh Stockdell, Alexander Donnan Hamilton, Joseph Dunn Osborne, Churchill Gibson Chamberlayne, James Hamilton, Alston Hamilton, David Meade Mann, James Mann, Gordon McCabe, Jr.,

John Patterson Madison, T. S. Beckwith, Jr., James Mullen, Robert D. Budd — and so on through one hundred and fifty names."

And so the roll of honor went on. Honor is the key word.

The small wooden building which housed the school has been torn down. But the foundation, the words with which the Old Man closed his address before examinations, survives.

On a granite marker are these words: "You cannot all be scholars, but you can all be gentlemen."

SUNDAY

❁

CHURCH BELLS, some impinging on others, different tunes but the same call to worship. Petersburg is a city of churches and church-goers.

During the Siege — 1864-65 — when General Lee was in the city and General Grant waiting to get in, church going was something of a hazard from bursting shells.

General Lee went to St. Paul's Church, and "Traveller" could be seen on Sunday morning tethered to the old iron fence.

As the Siege progressed a serious condition arose. The ladies were afraid to venture out to church! So the city fathers put it to General Meade of the Union army that church attendance was falling off. He ordered a "cease-fire" for the hours of ten to one on Sunday, and the ladies went peacefully to church, unarmed, except for parasols against the summer sun.

Sunday began with Salley Lunn. A fluted, brown mound of bread on the breakfast table. This was accompanied by fried oysters in the "R" months — not pale conglomerate lumps of batter — but individual delicious nuggets. Everything has an individual flavor in Petersburg, even oysters.

After breakfast we went to church. We wore our Sunday silks or Sunday suits, and our best hats. We walked in the pre-motor age, but now many people ride. And if you want to, just stand on the corner — any corner — you will not need your thumb — just look pleasant and wear your best hat.

After church we had mid-day dinner. The best china, a long white damask cloth, with an embroidered, lace-trimmed centrepiece, and a bowl of flowers in the middle.

The napkins matched the tablecloth, and the napkin rings matched us. Big silver ones for the grown-ups, and smaller ones for the small-fry — or maybe a wooden one, a souvenir of someone's travels.

My aunt and the ham were at one end of the table, my uncle and a huge platter of fried chicken at the other. He served the plates, we passed them — assaying the importance of the person by the piece.

I sat next to my uncle, who was raised in a family predominantly feminine. I noticed that he always wound up with some odd bits — a neck or back, and a gizzard. I asked him if he didn't like the breast, and he said, "Bless you, I never tasted one!"

Ladies got the breast, boys got the drumstick, and all of us got the fluffy potatoes. (A meal was practically nude without potatoes.) There was creamy corn pudding (no sugar, please) and butter beans (not limas) and cucumbers so thin you could see through them, and smelling as cool as the ice in the bowl, floating round with the vinegar and pepper on top.

Sunday was a special day, and Sunday food different from week-day menus. The main dish was apt to be fowl, or a delicate sort of meat, like lamb or veal. Roast beef didn't come to Sunday dinner. Neither did some vegetables — cabbage didn't come. Perhaps it was not sufficiently refined — cauliflower was more appropriate. But, of course, as Mark Twain remarked, cauliflower was cabbage with a college education.

Hot desserts — brown betty, blackberry roll, apple dumplings, were taboo on Sunday. In fact, it had not been too long since anything hot was not for Sunday consumption. This stemmed, of course, from the days when everybody, cooks included, went to church. No mundane food was allowed to interfere with spiritual needs.

The dessert was apt to be a light and fluffy affair; Spanish cream, jelly and custard, charlotte russe. Best of all, of course, was ice cream. This was the end toward which dinners (like creation) moved. Peach, perhaps, unless it was my birthday and I could choose my favorite — burnt sugar.

Kenna, Kennard Crawley Jefferson, a butler as fine as his name, and a gentleman of the old, or *any*, school, froze the ice cream. In the shade of the mulberry tree, on the cellar steps, he and the freezer joined hands. Grind, grind — a slight squawk — grind, grind, slowing down as the ice cream got hard — g-r-i-n-d — a wonderful Sunday sound.

Our sense of timing (there were several children in the house) was remarkable. We always appeared just in time to lick the dasher. If a blob fell out on the brick walk we almost cried. Then the freezer was packed — more ice, more salt, an old piece of carpet on top — and there it sat in wooden dignity until dessert. And no tray pulled out of a mechanical freezer ever made ice cream like this!

TABB STREET PRESBYTERIAN CHURCH — Once capped by a steeple, this church was dedicated in January, 1844. The removal of the steeple left it a fine example of Greek Revival architecture, a style popular in Petersburg.

Sunday afternoons we took walks and read Sunday books. These we got from the Sunday School Library — the *Elsie* books were familiar guests. Or perhaps Bible stories were read to us, or some favorite Christmas present like "Apples of Gold in Pictures of Silver." The "apples" never lost their savor, nor the gold its shining glow.

The grown-ups were busy with Church papers: *The Southern Churchman,* the *Richmond Christian Advocate,* the *Religious Herald* (Baptist), the *Catholic Friend,* and the *Central Presbyterian.*

Sunday newspapers were taboo in some homes. I shall never forget a remark made by one of the great ladies of yesterday at the Armistice after the First World War. The news (not authentic) came Saturday that the war was over. On Sunday we waited breathless to hear the rumor verified. So did the great lady. "My dear, she confessed, "for the first time in fifty years I've read a profane newspaper on Sunday!"

This adjective was no reflection on the august journal I found her reading — any newspaper not of a religious nature was "profane."

On Sunday afternoon, friends dropped in — after their naps, of course. On cool days we would sit in front of the wood fire in the library. The parlor was something on the stiff side, like the New England "plush parlor." Ours ran to haircloth, that usually needed a shave, and the sofa was skiddy as a ski course.

The library was warm, mellow, with tall walnut bookcases filled with the classics, read *to* us and then *by* us.

My uncle liked to read aloud. He had a good voice, and I remember the fine rolling periods, the excitement of knights as they came clashing out of the rustling pages — with the added attraction of the nuts I was cracking, and the apples my aunt peeled for us with her folding silver knife.

In the library there was, of course, a center table, with a graceful chandelier above with curved ribbons of linked brass, leading to the crystal shades for the gas light. There were lace curtains, stiff as boards, and warm, red over-draperies, tied back with cords with big, long tassels — fun to plait.

Every new visitor enlarged the circle in front of the fire (Kate, bring another chair for Aunt Lillie and Miss Jessie) — we brought more, and less comfortable ones, from the parlor. These were straight-backed, but so were the ladies. Ladies did not loll — the chair back, and milady's back were both unbending, and never the twain should meet.

The talk went on, leisurely talk — the ladies and the glowing logs gossiping softly together.

The gentlemen smoked, but the ladies — heaven forbid! Liquor and tobacco were for gentlemen only.

After the last guest had been shown out, with admonition to "Come soon," and the grandfather clock had struck seven, we fixed supper.

This meant finding something in the ice-box — delving down under the blanket that covered the precious ice — and some left-overs in the pantry.

We toasted the bread. This we did with a long toasting fork in front of the grate fire in the dining room. When our faces got red, and the bread got brown, we were ready.

There was ham, of course, and preserves. This was apt to be damsons, or maybe cherries, glowing in the old red dish.

After supper, we gathered around the piano and sang hymns — yes, we did. And very nice it was, too — perhaps some of us were a little off key, but there was sweet concord as we upheld a tradition. We finished with "Now the day is over."

Yes, that day is over.

And I wish it weren't.

THE OLD KITCHEN

HE KITCHEN was a big room connected with the house by a porch — or in some cases even out in the yard. These were generally equipped with hot and cold running children to get the food to the dining room intact.

Our kitchen was a place of lovely smells. Bread baking in the oven, pickle spicing in the jar, and ham browning from honey to amber in the huge, old, fat, black stove, sitting in hooded dignity.

I miss the warmth and friendliness of the old stove — flames belching out when we lifted the lid to poke in another piece of wood — or the rose-red embers of coke for toasting, or broiling chops.

It is hard to warm up to the smug, white and chromium range — an introvert and a pale personality. I have much sympathy for the old-time cook who said, "No 'lectric stove gwine brown the biscuits."

She also lost confidence in the mechanical refrigerator — a fairly new-comer to Petersburg. When a friend [who had the habit of emptying the ice cubes in the tray to enlarge the supply], failed to do this one day, Liza came to her much disturbed, "Deed, Miss Rosa, something's the matter with that 'friji-dijus' — 'tain't laid a piece of ice today!"

The kitchen was warm and friendly. It had no more resemblance to the modern kitchenette than a blacksmith shop to a garage.

In the middle of our kitchen was an enormous table, scrubbed to a snowy whiteness, a nice contrast to the black stove gleaming with "spit and polish." There were huge pots and a soapstone griddle for making the cornmeal batter cakes with brown lace edges. Mighty good with herring roe (Liza, be sure to put some herrings in soak).

A young visitor from up North was enjoying this menu one morning, then said it was the first time he'd ever eaten caviar for breakfast.

A shocked silence greeted this remark. No wonder — herring is a demo-cratic dish and as far removed from caviar as Petersburg is from St. Peters-burg, "that *was*," as we say here.

There was a fluting iron in the corner — petticoats were wide and ruffled, and all had to be fluted.

The coffee grinder was nearby. We turned the handle, pulled open the drawer, and the odors of Araby poured out.

We had a biscuit block, of course — a huge trunk of a tree on stout legs, for beating biscuits. A sightseeing Yankee visitor to another old home was heard to remark that this "block" was used for beheading the slaves — we just made biscuits on ours.

The ham boiler, that noble vessel whose precious alchemy would turn an old black, slabsided ham into a thin rose-red sliver of amber-rined meat, had a place of honor.

We always had a ham on hand. It was like having money in the bank. It was kept on the porch in the wood cupboard, with the pierced tin doors — the *safe,* an appropriate place for treasure.

Our menus were liable to have ham for breakfast and dinner and supper. Supper, that perfect end of a perfect day, was made for ham. And turnovers (the Boston Parker House roll) blown up to southern size — crusty on the top and bottom, fluffy in the middle — "better butter two."

For "comp'ny" supper we had broiled chicken, tomatoes stuffed with veal and ham, and Sally Lunn, that brown, fluted mound of heavenly bread. Someone should write a poem about southern breads. Someone has. Judge Anthony Keiley, a man of taste and distinction, wrote:

> Let the Irishman drink to Saint Patrick,
> St. George be the Englishman's cry,
> The Welshman fill up to St. David,
> Their toasts are all perfect — but I
> Will fill up my glass
> And drink to the lass
> The sweetest one under the sun,
> The lass who is able
> To sit at the table
> And pass her own Sally Lunn.

THE MARKET — *This graceful building was built 1878-79. It is the fourth structure to occupy the site which has been used as a market center since 1787.*

No alarm clock was needed to get us up in the morning — the beat, beat, beat, in the kitchen, as Liza made the biscuits, did that. They came to the table, hot, a light beige color — small and delicious and habit forming.

And, of course, there were waffles. Some of these were square, made in the old molds that came from the Tredegar Iron Works in Richmond, the arsenal of the Confederacy. No matter what the shape, they were very light, very crusty — the butter forming little golden pools as it melted — "Well, yes, I believe I could eat *one* more."

After breakfast by aunt "gave out." This was not as serious as it sounds. It meant giving out supplies for the day's menus.

There was a rendezvous between my aunt, the keybasket and the cook. The keybasket was an important part of a Virginia lady's accessories. It was fairly large, with a handle, made of embossed leather, or patent leather, stitched in an intricate design. It also was ambulatory — it was always where my aunt wasn't. If she was upstairs, it was downstairs, or the other way around, and I was up-ing and down-ing in between.

"Giving out" began in the storeroom. Sugar, lard, meal with two eggs sitting on top for the batterbread, and other supplies. Plans for the day's meals were discussed, with particular attention, mine at least, to dessert.

Dinner was a midday affair. Six o'clock dinner was greeted with uplifted eyebrows — no sense to it — just putting on airs.

We didn't put on airs, we just put dinner on the table anywhere from two to three o'clock, and afterward everybody took a nap.

There wasn't much else we *could* do, after the roast, the turnip salad, the corn pone — hot, thin and brown, with buttermilk, and winding up with the blackberry roll.

This came on pale but interesting when cut, the purple juice oozing out to mix with the hard sauce — that delectable creamy stuff made with sugar and butter, beaten to a fluff with just enough brandy to make you want more.

Sometimes the "wait-and-see" (which we were told to curb our curiosity about dessert) was brown betty, baked apple dumplings, bread pudding, or grated sweet potato pudding, served with a dollop of damson preserves on the side.

Of course, all this meant a good cook. And when I say "good" I give the word many connotations.

Our cook, Liza, presided over the kitchen — presided is the word. She had dignity, wisdom, and a great kindness.

One day I went, as I often did, to the kitchen for comfort and advice. The smell of cooking was delicious — "Liza, what smells so good — ham?"

"Yes'm," she opened the oven door to baste the clove-starred beauty simmering in wine-red juices . . . "Yes'm, it does have a downright hamish smell!"

I sat at the table, and as usual, dumped my worries in Liza's ample lap.

She listened quietly, then laid aside the long-handled spoon (and my worries) in one graceful gesture of her bare, brown arm. Then, reaching back into her experience, and from the deep wisdom of her race, she gave her recipe for living — " 'Tis best to learn to wear life like a loose garment."

CHRISTMAS

❊

ETERSBURG, like any great lady, fits her mood to the occasion. At Christmas she is at her gayest and most hospitable best. Tradition, that minstrelsy of the past, sings
through the preparations.

In the old days we "got ready" long before the great day.
Something we called "Christmas in our bones" permeated the atmosphere.
Balls of bright wool fell out of ladies' laps to make a rainbow on the rug.
Afghans were knitted, "fascinators" crocheted to delight the feminine heart.
Bits of linen were stretched on embroidery hoops to make a center-piece —
gay skeins of silk made flowers to rival nature's own.

And handkerchiefs! They were initialed by hand as long as eye-sight and
the Christmas list held out. ("A linen handkerchief is always acceptable and
in good taste.")

Good taste with the Santa Claus set meant something different — mostly
cakes and candies.

First of all, fruit cake. One of the first signs of the approach of the holiday
season was the fruit for the Christmas cakes drying before the fire. Huge
white platters with currants and raisins were set to dry on the wide black
fender. And very exciting this was, too, when ashes came powdering down,
and small chunks of coal as black and shiny as the currants, to say nothing
of scraps of paper thrown at the fire, but landing in the fruit.

All the preparations for Christmas sweets went on in the dining room at
my great-grandfather's old home. This long, low-ceiled room was two steps
down from the more modern part of the house. At one end was the mantel,
so high that I could never reach up to the fat blue vases on either end, or peek
into the long mirror that nearly covered it. On one side of the room was an
old walnut side-board with a fox's head on top. Opposite was a window with
red geraniums and begonias in front of the white frilly curtains, and above,
iron brackets with green and purple glasses with water hyacinths in them.
A grandfather clock stood sentinel in the corner, and in the middle of the

room was the table, loaded at this time with the "makings" of the fruit cakes. Flour, sugar, the scales, papers for lining fluted pans with the smokestack in the center, eggs — ah, even now I can see the whites changing from foam to snow, and hear (but never see) what was going on where the yolks were being creamed in the yellow bowl. The "beater" always tilted the bowl, and no matter how I tiptoed I never got over the top. No latter-day mystery story, no thriller, has ever seemed so alluring to me as "The Case of the Yellow Bowl."

In front of the fire sat the aunts cutting the fruit. Black worsted skirts were turned back to keep from being scorched by the flame. This revealed snowy petticoats with tucked and fluted frills discreetly covering high, black button shoes.

In the firelight the citron turned to gold and almonds slithered into bits of pearl. But the coconut was prettiest of all as it was grated into mounds of snow. I took a little taste, then a few almonds, a few more raisins and a handful of currants — alas!

"Kate" (my aunt turned suddenly), "put those currants back. I declare there won't be enough left for the cake!"

"Yes'm," I subsided meekly, but momentarily. The citron rind nobody could blame me for taking. Nobody did, but I discovered the horrid economic principle of supply and demand. If they don't want it, you don't, either.

At last the batter is mixed, so knobby and stiff, and, unlike nature in the raw, not only mild, but delightful. The last delectable smells are added from the bottles in the bottom of the sideboard, and I'm given the bowl to lick. An exciting experience. I finally emerged with most of the batter on my face, but with enough inside to be sure that at prayers that evening my uncle (I thought) prayed to be *"unpainedly"* thankful — I know I did.

Next day came the white fruit cake with the odor of rose water and bitter almond rising like incense. Then the lesser cakes; snowballs, nice because there was so much icing, and Naples biscuit, long, narrow sponge cakes. These were not very exciting, but all right if you couldn't do any better. They were useful for sending out on trays to friends — particularly to ladies in delicate health.

These trays (which we called *waiters*) were a feature of the holidays. They went out and they came in. There would come a ring at the bell and we would race down the hall to open the door. A large, fat black person with a large, fat white waiter greeted us. We would peep under the snowy napkin — rose, thin slices of ham, white mounds of breast of turkey, beaten biscuit, Spanish cream with wheat and corn sculptured in gold jelly on top, and cakes — such entrancing cakes.

Next in interest to cakes came custards — the sweet potato custards, coconut custards — delightful individual pies. I wonder if there is a pie line that runs along with the Mason and Dixon? So many Virginia pies are called by another name. However, nothing could be as sweet, or as indigestibly interesting as our citron puddings. I happened on the recipe in an old cook book, dated 1853. "Yolks of eight eggs, three-quarters of a pound of sugar, one-quarter of a pound of butter, two tablespoons of cracker, soaked in a teacup of new milk, and a glass of wine and a little nutmeg; all well-beaten and poured over sliced citron in a rich paste." There you are; and may you be "unpainedly thankful."

At last, it is Christmas eve, though I had begun to think it never would be. The old clock had poked along unbelievably. But now it seemed to be doing better, being gaily decorated with holly and running cedar. The sideboard had a wreath around the fox's head, dangling rakishly over one ear, and the pink and gold pitchers on either end were filled with mistletoe.

A big clothes hamper was overflowing with gaily-tied presents to be distributed and our stockings . . . But let me explain that when I say stockings, I mean long, ribbed, much-darned and somewhat faded cotton stockings, not the effete red and white trifles of today. (Mine were so short that I borrowed one from the tallest boy.)

Finally, I was tucked into a high mahogany bed, the firelight flickering over my empty stocking dangling from the bell knob by the mantel, where I expected (and usually found) a pink silk dolly tucked in the top.

On Christmas in the early morning, when the little boys were starting out and the big boys coming in, I made the grand lunge for my stocking and turned it upside down on the bed — the nicest present was always in the toe.

Then the wild excitement of opening the presents — and then church. That meant sweet smell of cedar, the lovely, shiny star: "O Little Town of Bethlehem." Someway, we got through the sermon with many clinkings of the new lock-bracelet, surreptitious pats of new gloves and hankies, and openings and shuttings of the tiny red purse with the gold pennies.

We raced home where leaves were being put in the already long table. But not long enough, for even with extra places the younger children had to sit at the side table. This was something of a tragedy since no matter how mountainous the ice cream looked when it appeared in the pantry door, it always dwindled to a pathetic peak when it got to us.

The turkey! The early settler who claimed that the turkey was a "moughty onconvenient bird — a little too much for one and not quite enough for two" did not dine with big families in the old days.

On a huge platter, Kenna, the butler, with his black face almost as shiny as the turkey, would deposit the bird in front of my uncle. Tall and dignified, he rose and the carving began, turning into an engineering feat as he tunneled for stuffing. And then the important question: "Light bread or corn bread?"

That meant which dressing — from the north or wheat bread and celery end, or the south or corn bread end. And let me advise you right now that whether you belong to the oyster or chestnut school, always say "corn bread" when you have the chance. Crumbly and with gravy on the side and a sausage-cake hat on top, this is just how the well-turned-out turkey should be dressed.

The carving goes on and at last my uncle sinks into his chair — a moment too soon. One of the boys' plates is back for a second serving. "Bless my soul!" — my uncle pretends shocked surprise — "Son, you back again already?" But he laughs as he gets up and turns the turkey over. I've often wondered when the carver ever ate — the second flight followed so closely on the first.

This part of the dinner for the "side table," however, was, to go along with Mr. Browning, only the first for which the last was made. At last, the final plate is taken off, the remaining crumb crumbed and Kenna comes in with the fruit cakes and this time the question before the house is "black or white?"

After perhaps a little of both, we come on down through the custards and the puddings to my aunt's end of the table with the bowl of jelly in the ruby glass dish, cream ruffling around the edge in a fluffy collar. As the jelly slithers from bowl to plate we try to decide between that and Spanish cream — finally leaving it to the arbiter of "eeny-meeny-miney-mo."

The nuts are in the old silver cake basket, there is an epergne of fruit, and chunks of cheese in the green majolica leaf dish. And then the final excitement of Kenna's appearance with the plum pudding all ablaze.

At last, we totter into the library — and the people from the northeast corner of the table rush over to the flaming logs to warm their almost frozen feet. No wonder they take their coffee standing, revolving happily before the fire as they thaw out.

After a much-needed nap, the gentlemen start out on the egg-nog rounds. The whole street is an open house. Behind each wide door there is a happy gathering with the host or hostess presiding over the yellow bowl of egg-nog — of course, a punch bowl *would* do. As each guest is ladled out a foamy cup, he declares — *always* — that it is the best — the *very* best, he's ever tasted, and he must have the recipe.

The rounds continue with my uncle winding up with a party of delightful silver heads much like his own. With their cheeks getting pinker, their eyes brighter, as they have "just one more." They talk about the war — they reminisce — "I recollect . . ." a veteran begins.

If they recollected too long, my aunt would send some of us to escort my uncle home. One afternoon they let me go. It was snowing. A gentle veil dropped its quietness over the old city.

In a Victorian home a party of gentlemen were seated around a table with a red felt cover on it. In the middle of the table was a big bowl of egg-nog, and in front of each guest, a silver cup.

In the place of honor was an open Bible. The gentlemen were discussing a passage of Scripture.

The firelight glinted on silver heads and silver cups. The Good Book, good cheer, men of good will — God rest ye, merry gentlemen.

Christmas night after the last pop cracker has popped and the final rocket has written its starry message on the sky, we gather in the library.

The fire has glowed to purple embers, and someone finds the long wax taper to light the chandelier, prisms twinkling and tinkling. The circle widens as the late comers drift in, and then my uncle begins to read. Yes, you guessed it. "Tiny Tim" of yesterday and today and tomorrow.

Soft light falls on the listening heads, silver, brown and blonde, slick little-boy heads and fluffy little-girl heads, soft dark "crimps" and white "crimps."

My uncle looks around the circle — his folks. But gaps are beginning to show — he clears his throat — pauses, then gallantly his voice rings out in the words of "Tiny Tim": "God bless us every one!"

A white handkerchief comes out with a flourish, my uncle's eyes turn to the diminutive dearness of his wife: "Madame," he takes off his glasses, "God bless my soul, something seems to be the matter with my specs."

POSTSCRIPT

POSTSCRIPT

❀

Old traditions for Christmas festivities still prevail in Petersburg. They add 'spice and spirit' to the happy season. Here they are:

EGG-NOG

1 dozen eggs
1 pint whipping cream
1 jigger whiskey and
1 tablespoon (level) sugar to each egg

(Much improved by the addition of 4 jiggers of brandy and 2 jiggers of rum.)

Beat egg yolks and sugar until thick and lemon colored. Whip cream. Very slowly add liquor to eggs, then whipped cream, and last fold in the stiffly beaten egg whites. Sprinkle with nutmeg, if desired.

APPLE TODDY

One peck Winesap apples — baked until well done, strain through sieve — sweeten well (about twice as sweet as for pie). Let stand until sugar is thoroughly dissolved. Add equal amount of good brandy — beating well into apple mixture. Good when made, but improves with age.

PICKLED OYSTERS

Cook one-half gallon oysters, half cup salt, until oysters curl on edges — strain and put on a block of ice to plump. To one pint vinegar, add pepper corns, mace, whole cloves and thinly sliced lemon to taste. Bring to a boil and pour over oysters. Put in jars and keep in a cool place. Small pickled red peppers are an addition.

WINE JELLY

One box shredded gelatine soaked in one pint cold water, dissolved in one quart boiling water. Boil with a stick of cinnamon, juice and rind of two lemons and two oranges. Strain and add one pound sugar and one pint of sherry wine and a dash of brandy. Keeps well.

127

BEEF A LA MODE

Remove bone and trim away tougher part around edges of a 10 or 12 pound round of beef. Bind roast with a stout piece of muslin — as wide as the roast is deep — tacking tightly. Have ready one pound fat salt pork cut in strips as wide as your finger. Pour over this one half pint vinegar, simmered, until it boils, with one onion chopped, two teaspoons prepared mustard, one teaspoon cloves, one half teaspoon allspice, one half teaspoon pepper, a bunch of herbs minced, a table-spoon sugar. With a long, slender knife, make incisions in the roast all the way through, about one inch apart. Lard the meat with pork strips which have remained in vinegar until cool. Add bread crumbs to vinegar remaining and pack into place where bone was removed. Also, rub crumbs (soaked) over top of the roast. Put in a roaster with a little water, cook with top on for one half hour to the pound. (Baste often.) Let cool in pan, and serve cold, thinly sliced.

FRUIT CAKE (White)

1 pound butter or substitute	*1 pound white raisins*
1 pound sugar	*2 coconuts, if small, 1 if large, grated*
1 pound flour	*1 teaspoon mace*
1 dozen eggs	*Grated rind and juice of 1 lemon*
1 pound citron	*One half cup whiskey*

Mix and bake in same manner as given for Fruit Cake (Dark).
Candied cherries and pineapple may be added.

SYLLABUB

Christmas was not complete without syllabub.

Cream — whipped — amount according to the thirst of your guests
Sugar, to taste
Sherry wine

This is a very light adjunct to Christmas festivities. How light is best told by an old Negro servitor who arrived (of course) at the pantry door on Christmas day.

She asked the Negro if he would like a cup. The old man drank it down, then commented: "Deed, mistis, if you gwine gimme a dram, gimme a dram — don't give me something jes' make me dream I had a dram!"

The lady of the house had just finished churning the cream and putting the finishing touches to a bowl of syllabub.

PLUM PUDDING

1 pound suet
One half pound bread crumbs
1 pound currants
1 pound raisins
One half pound shelled almonds
6 eggs
One half teaspoon salt
One half pound sugar
1 pint milk
2 teaspoons nutmeg
1 teaspoon mace
2 apples, finely chopped
1 cup flour (scant)
1 wine glass whiskey

Put suet through meat grinder, beat eggs separately, cream butter and sugar, add beaten egg yolks, flour the fruit well, and add all ingredients to the first mixture. Cover tightly and boil 4 hours. Serve with brandy poured over it and bring blazing to the table.

FRUIT CAKE (Dark)

1 pound butter or substitute
1 pound flour
1 dozen eggs
1 pound sugar
1 pound citron
1 pound almonds
1 pound currants
2 pounds seeded raisins
2 teaspoons mace
2 teaspoons nutmeg
1 cup whiskey

Cream butter with half the sugar, beat egg yolks with the rest of the sugar — combine with flour, fruit and nuts (*floured*) — adding stiffly beaten egg whites alternately with floured fruit and nuts. Lastly, add whiskey. Line funnel pan with greased paper before filling with the mixture. Put a pan of water beneath and above cake to cook in a slow oven about 4 hours or until straw comes out clean when stuck into the cake. Keep in tin box.

CHARLOTTE RUSSE

Take a box of gelatine and dissolve in cold water; then take three pints of milk, and beat the yolks of four eggs light, with half pound of white sugar; put it with the gelatine on the fire; stir until it boils, then put in a bowl to cool; when cold whip a quart of cream, and stir into custard gradually; put in molds, lined with sponge cake.

TRIFLE
(OR TIPSY PARSON)

In the bottom of a glass bowl place bits of sponge cake, cut in squares; small pieces of citron preserves, cut into thin slices, and interspersed with the cake; pour over the cake one gill of best Madeira or sherry; then fill the bowl within half inch of top with a rich custard; lastly heap up on top whipped cream; sprinkle on top colored sugar. This makes a pretty dish.

SPANISH CREAM

Two quarts milk, eight eggs, three-quarters of a box of gelatine, two cups sugar; make as custard, after dissolving the gelatine; when cold add whites of eggs beaten to a stiff froth; serve with whipped cream, flavored with sherry wine.

PARTIAL BIBLIOGRAPHY

❦

BOOKS AND ARTICLES

Bernard, George S.: *War Talks of Confederate Veterans.*

Brooks, Jerome E.: *The Mighty Leaf; Tobacco Through the Centuries.*

Claiborne, John Herbert: *Seventy-five Years in Old Virginia.*

Corti, Egon Caesar: *History of Smoking.*

Davis, Arthur Kyle: *Three Centuries of an Old Virginia Town.*

Freeman, Douglas Southall: *R. E. Lee, a Biography.*

Gordon, Armistead C.: *Memories and Memorials of William Gordon McCabe.*

Gregory, Edward S.: *A Sketch of the History of Petersburg.*

Machen, Arthur: *Anatomy of Tobacco.*

Pollock, Edward S.: *Historical and Industrial Guide to Petersburg, Virginia.*

Robert, Joseph C.: *Story of Tobacco in America.*

Robert, Joseph C.: *The Tobacco Kingdom.*

Scott, James G., and Edward A. Wyatt, IV: *Petersburg's Story.*

Todkill, Anas: *My Lady Pokahontas, With Notes by John Esten Cooke.*

Williamson, J. Pinckney: *Ye Olden Times, History of Petersburg.*

Wyatt, Edward A., IV: *Along Petersburg Streets.*

PERIODICALS

Northington, Oscar F.: *Taverns of Old Petersburg, William and Mary College Quarterly, 1936.*

Wyatt, Edward A., IV: *Rise of Industry in Ante-Bellum Petersburg, William and Mary College Quarterly Historical Magazine, January 1937.*

NEWSPAPERS

Grant's Petersburg Progress, 1865.

Petersburg Progress-Index, 1941.

Richmond Times-Dispatch, 1936.

The Southside Democrat, 1856.

OTHER PUBLICATIONS

Barton, Robert: *Plug Tobacco and Fine Art.*

Herndon, Melvin: *Tobacco in Colonial Virginia.*

Hill, Althea W.: *Christmas Traditions.*

Old Virginia Cook Book.

Quartermaster Training Command, Fort Lee, Virginia: *Fort Lee in the Historic Heartland of America.*

Requiescat In Pace

KATHARINE COPELAND ROBERTSON

18 February 1961

Design and Lithography:
WHITTET & SHEPPERSON, RICHMOND, VIRGINIA

Binding:
THE ALBRECHT COMPANY, BALTIMORE, MARYLAND

Paper:
SATURN BOOK

Type:
FAIRFIELD

Petersbur[g]

Appomattox River

Battersea

Peter Jones Trading Station

Strachan-Harrison House

High St.

To Dinwiddie

Tabb St Church

Folly Castle

Twin Houses

Wallace House

S. Market St.

Southern College

George Bolling House

McCabe House

Pocahontas Basin